Okay-okay! I know you're eager to start training but first let m

HOW TO USE THIS BOO

This book is divided into three parts:

1. Writing practice sheets for 174 Hanzi symbols required for Hanyu Shuiping Kaoshi (HSK) Level 1 test

The fact of the matter is that you'll probably have to use up a lot of practice paper before you memorize Chinese Hanzi symbols. This workbook is designed in a way that you can cut pages out of it and copy them as much as you like in a copying machine. Stroke order is provided for all of the listed Hanzi symbols.

2. Compound words writing practice

To become proficient in Chinese reading and writing it's not enough for you to learn individual Hanzi symbols. You would also need to know how to read and write words that are composed from several Hanzi symbols i.e. compound words. And what is a better way to learn those words than writing them down several times? The second part of the book is devoted to this. There're over 150 words with HSK Level 1 Hanzi symbols for you write along with some training sentences.

3. Cut out flash cards for 174 Hanzi symbols for HSK Level 1

Cut out these pages and then cut them again using cross marks. There you've got your own Hanzi flash cards with the symbol on one side and Pinyin reading on another. No need to spend extra on buying those fancy cardboard cards!

Let me not hold you any further!

让我们学习!

(Ràng wǒmen xuéxí!) Let's study!

We are happy to accept corrections and feedback regarding this workbook at:
lilas.publishing@ya.ru

Lilas Lingvo

Contents

的

Definition <u>possessive, adjectival suffix</u>
Pinyin de

的	的	的	白	白	白	的	的	的			

Definition <u>one; a, an; alone</u>
Pinyin yī

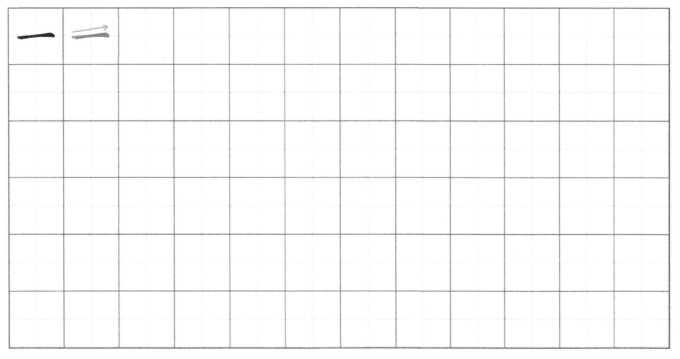

Definition indeed, yes, right; to be; demonstrative pronoun, this, that

Pinyin shì

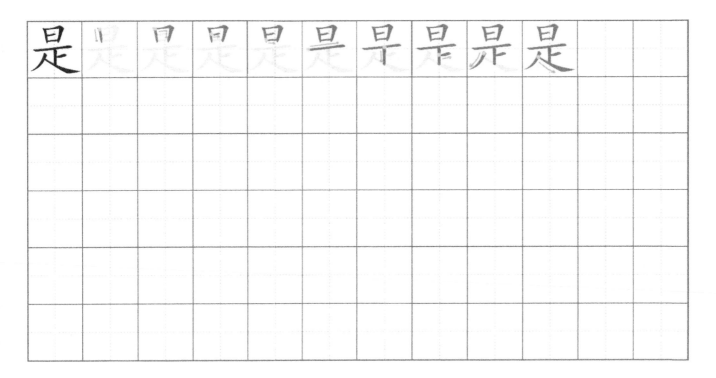

Definition no, not; un-; negative prefix

Pinyin bù

是,不

Definition <u>to finish; particle of completed action</u>

Pinyin le

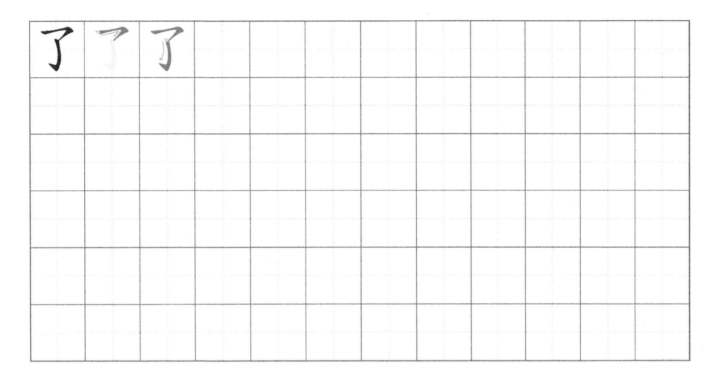

Definition <u>be at, in, on; consist in, rest</u>

Pinyin zài

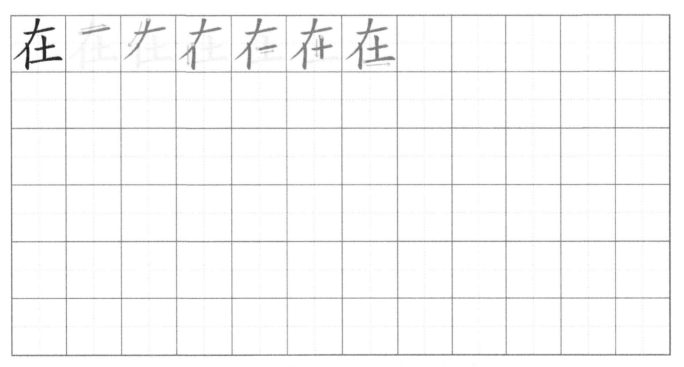

Definition   man; people; mankind; someone else

Pinyin   rén

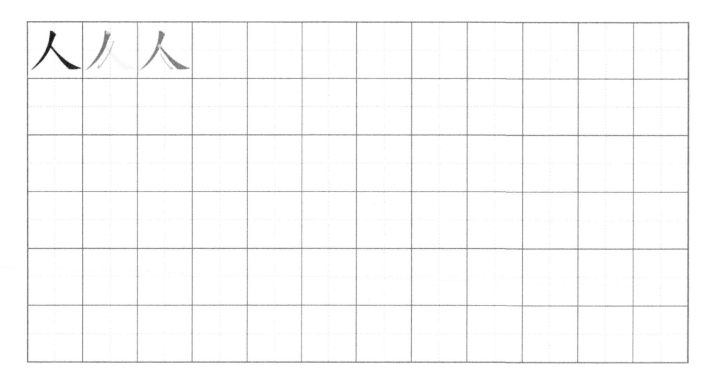

Definition   have, own, possess; exist

Pinyin   yǒu

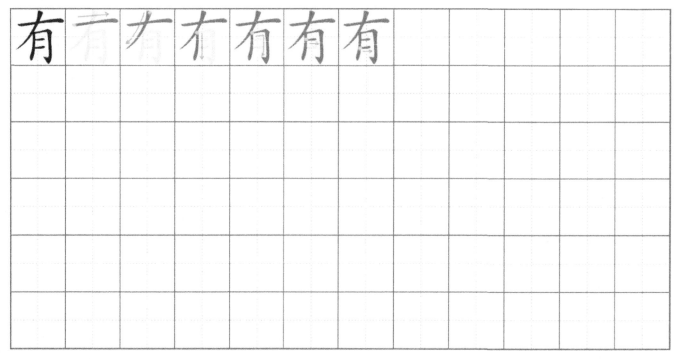

人,有   4

Definition <u>our, us, i, me, my, we</u>

Pinyin wǒ

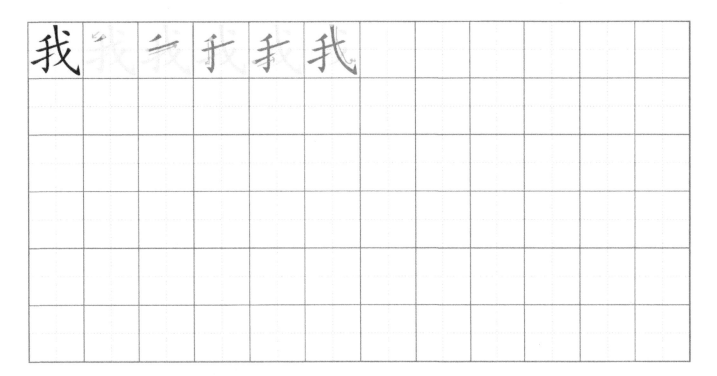

他

Definition <u>other, another; he, she, it</u>

Pinyin tā

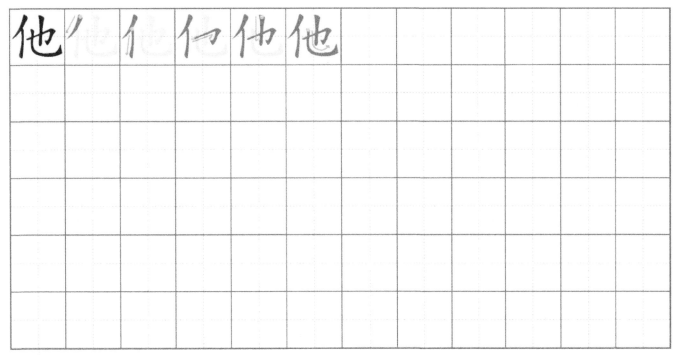

Definition <u>this, the, here</u>

Pinyin zhè

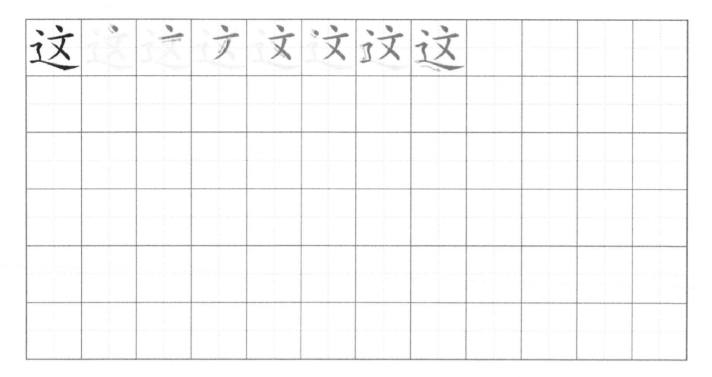

Definition <u>numerary adjunct, piece; single</u>

Pinyin gè

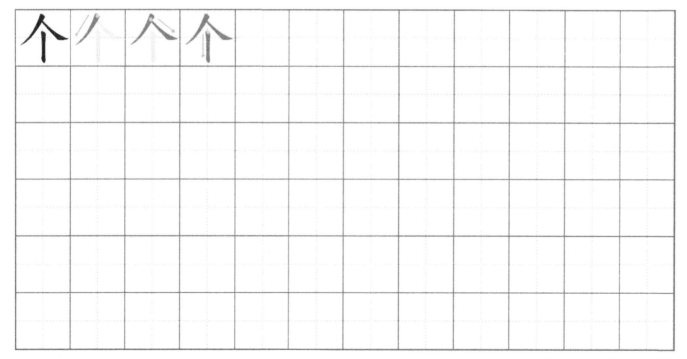

Definition   <u>adjunct pronoun indicate plural</u>

Pinyin   men

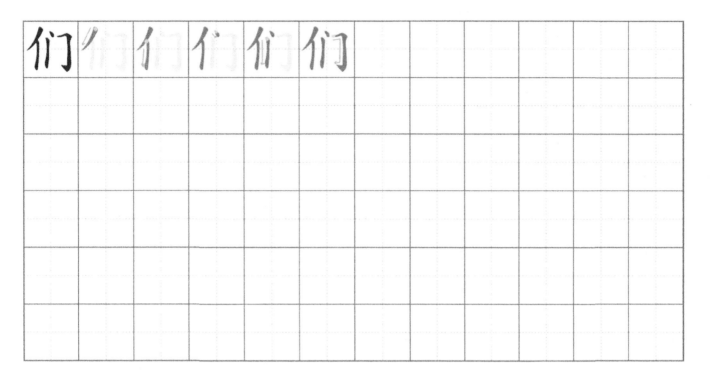

Definition   <u>central; center, middle; in the midst of;</u>
<u>hit (target); attain</u>

Pinyin   zhōng

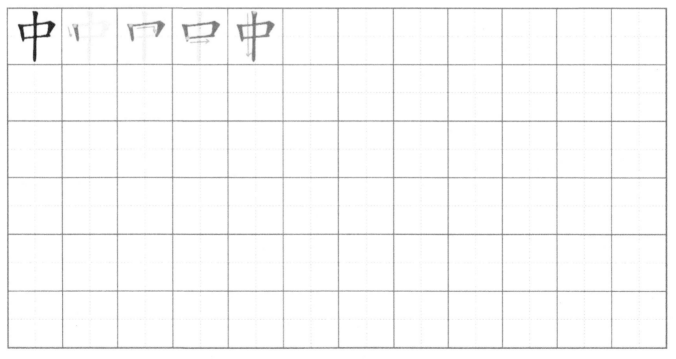

Definition come, coming; return, returning

Pinyin lái

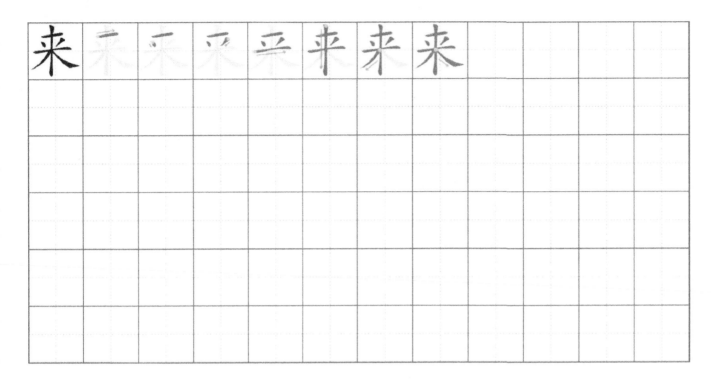

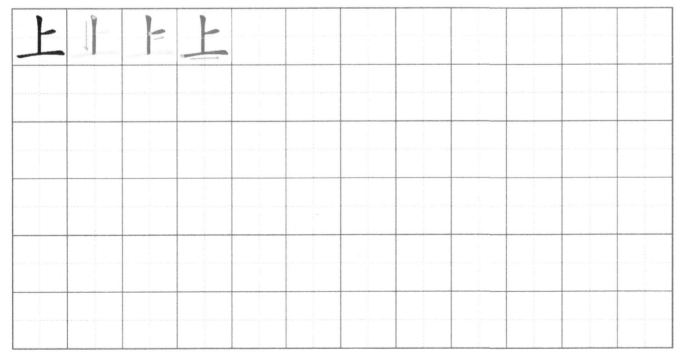

Definition top; superior, highest; go up, send up

Pinyin shàng

Definition big, great, vast, large, high
Pinyin dà

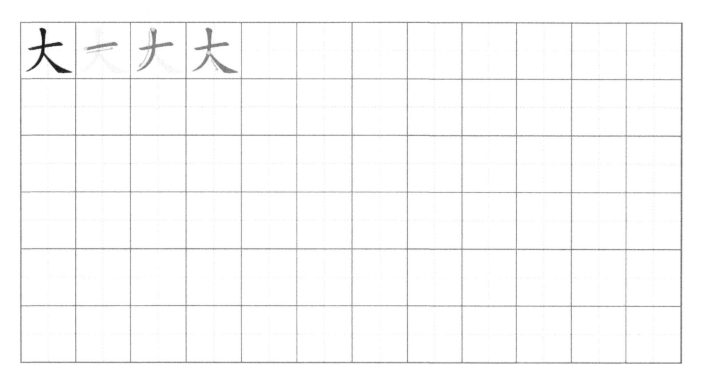

Definition harmony, peace; peaceful, calm
Pinyin hé

Definition <u>nation, country, nation-state</u>

Pinyin guó

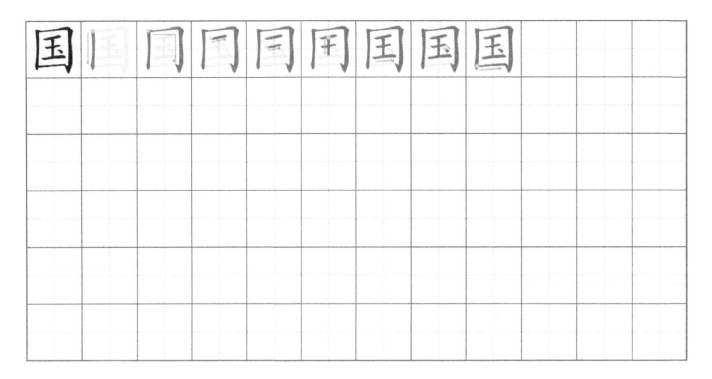

Definition <u>speak, say, talk; scold, upbraid</u>

Pinyin shuō

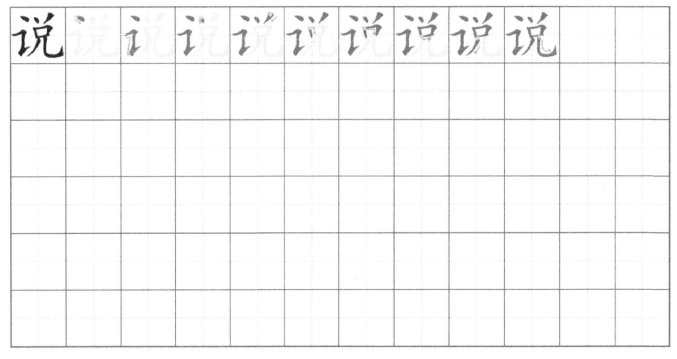

国,说

Definition time, season; era, age, period
Pinyin shí

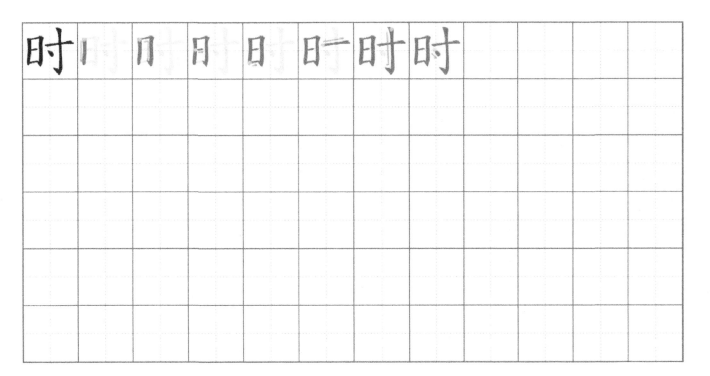

Definition go out, send out; stand; produce
Pinyin chū

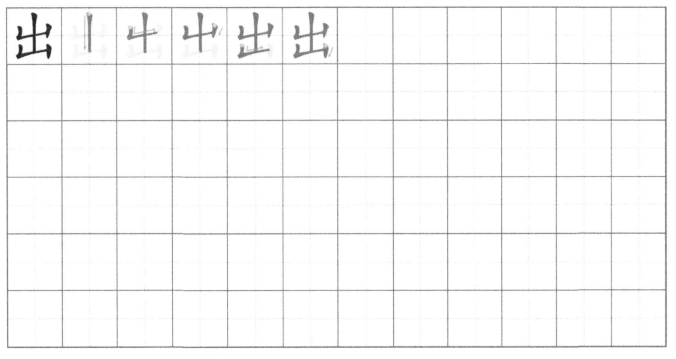

Definition assemble, meet together; meeting

Pinyin huì

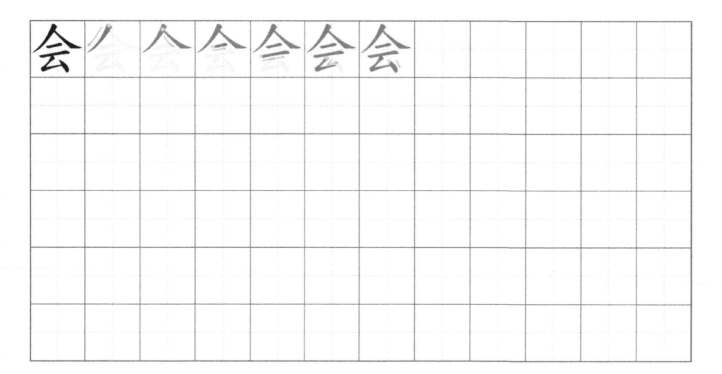

Definition you, second person pronoun

Pinyin nǐ

会,你

Definition correct, right; facing, opposed

Pinyin duì

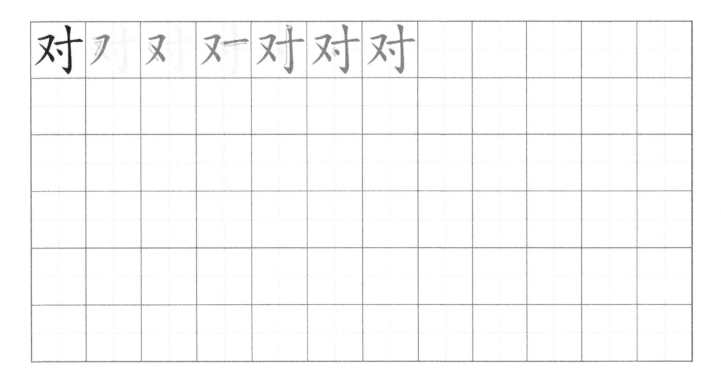

Definition life, living, lifetime; birth

Pinyin shēng

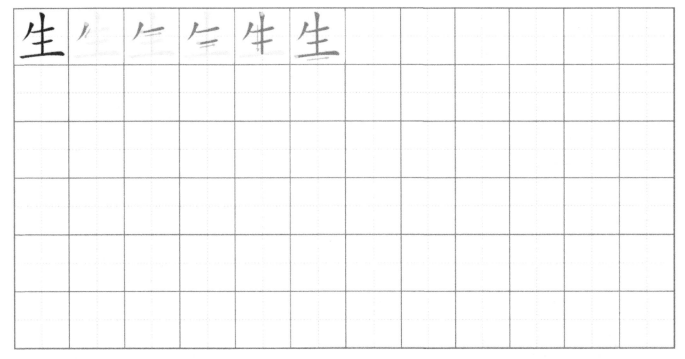

Definition <u>to be able; can, permitted to; ability</u>

Pinyin néng

能 能 能 能 能 能 能 能 能 能 能

Definition <u>offspring, child; fruit, seed of; 1st terrestrial branch</u>

Pinyin zi

子 了 了 子

能,子

Definition <u>that, that one, those</u>

Pinyin nà

Definition <u>under, underneath, below; down; inferior; bring down</u>

Pinyin xià

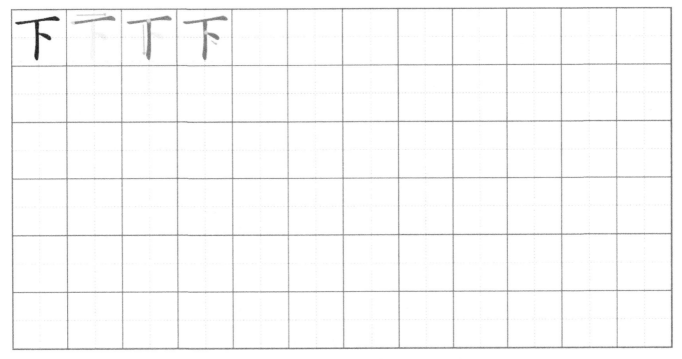

Definition year

Pinyin nián

Definition queen, empress, sovereign; (simp. for 口) behind, rear, after

Pinyin hòu

Definition make; work; compose, write; act, perform

Pinyin zuò

作	作	作	作	作	作	作	作			

Definition unit of distance; village; lane

Pinyin lǐ

里	里	里	里	里	里	里	里			

Definition house, home, residence; family

Pinyin jiā

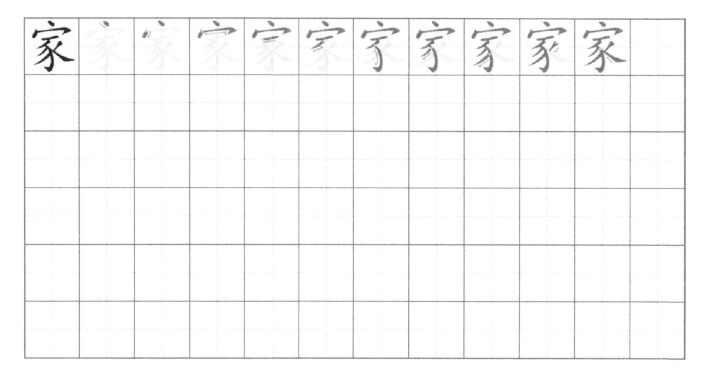

Definition much, many; more than, over

Pinyin duō

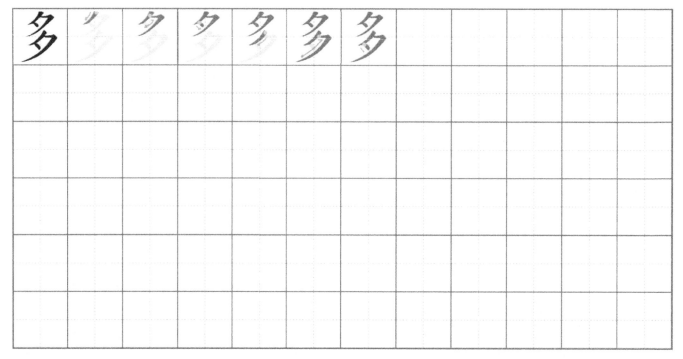

家,多

18

Definition <u>interrogative particle; repetition of a tune small;</u>
<u>tender</u>

Pinyin me

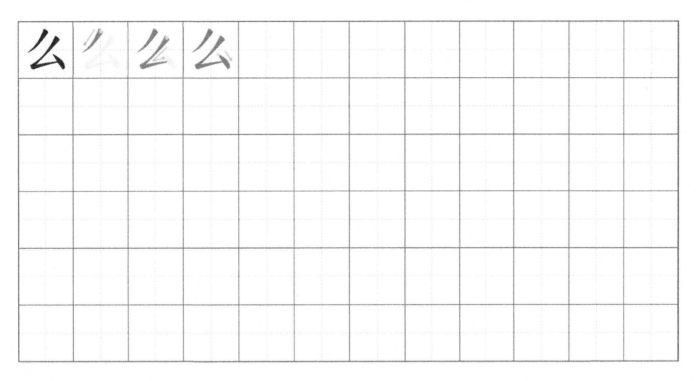

Definition <u>go away, leave, depart</u>

Pinyin qù

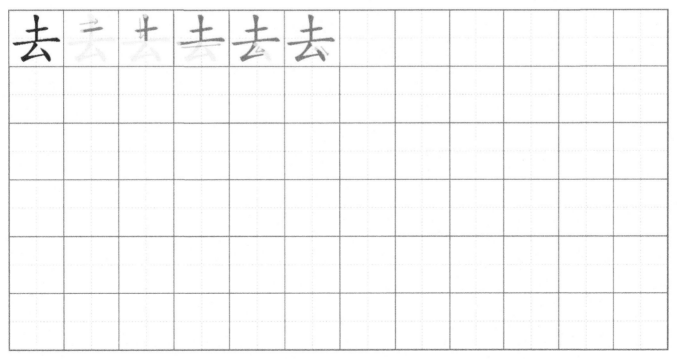

么,去   19   HSK1 Chinese Writing Workbook

Definition   learning, knowledge; school

Pinyin   xué

Definition   metropolis, capital; all, the whole; elegant, refined

Pinyin   dōu

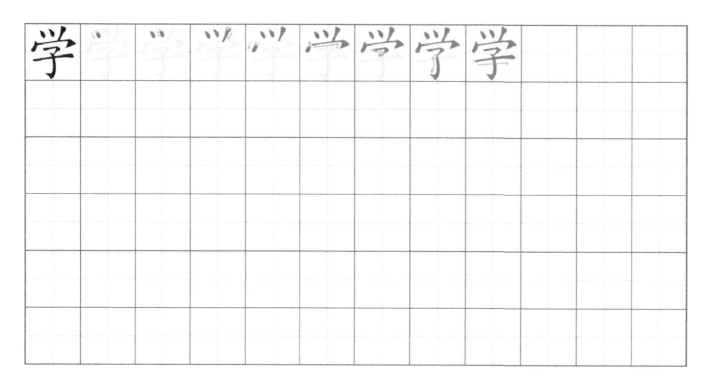

学,都

Definition <u>same, similar; together with</u>
Pinyin tóng

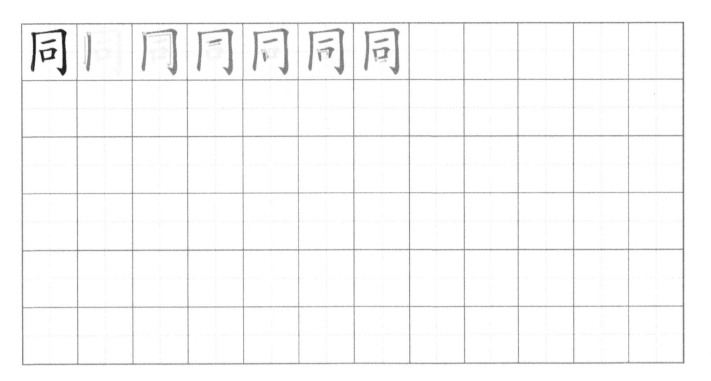

Definition <u>appear, manifest, become visible</u>
Pinyin xiàn

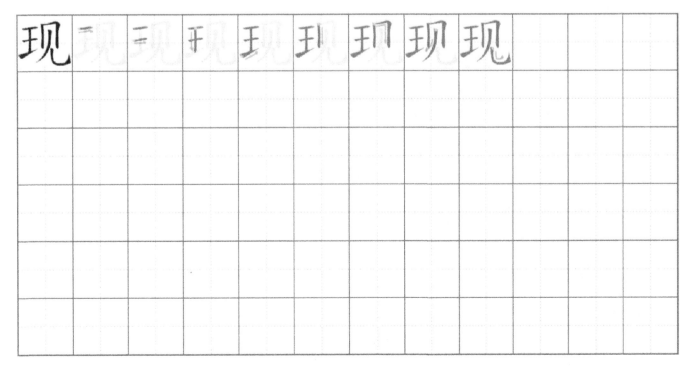

Definition   not, have not, none; drown, sink

Pinyin   méi

Definition   face; surface; plane; side, dimension

Pinyin   miàn

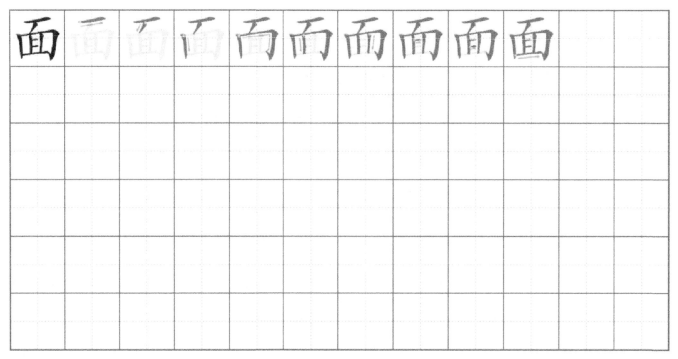

没,面

Definition <u>rise, stand up; go up; begin</u>

Pinyin qǐ

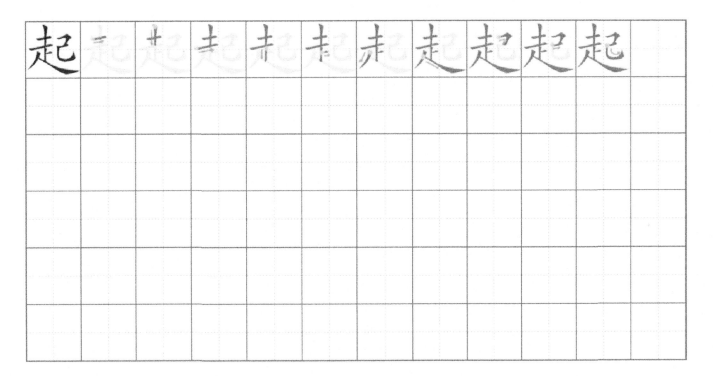

Definition <u>look, see; examine, scrutinize</u>

Pinyin kàn

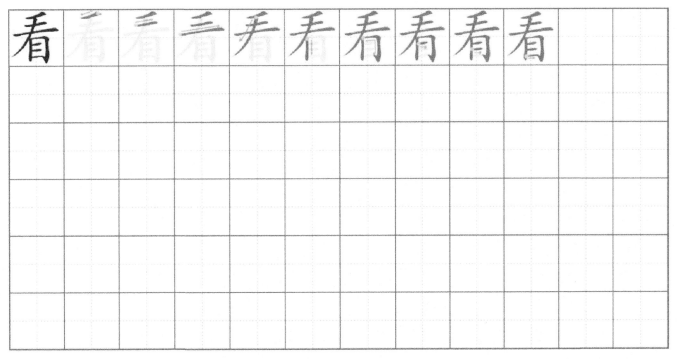

Definition <u>sky, heaven; god, celestial</u>

Pinyin tiān

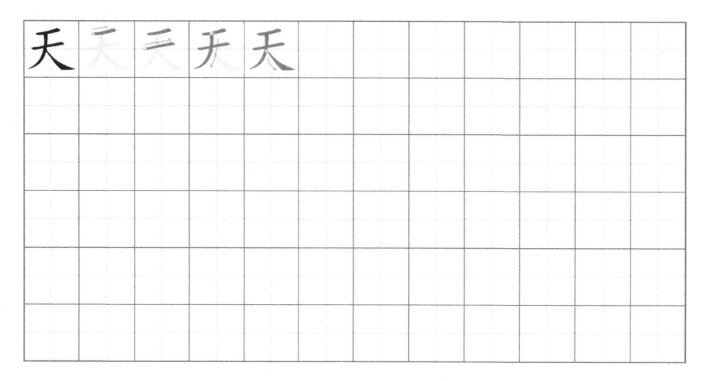

Definition <u>divide; small unit of time etc.</u>

Pinyin fēn

天,分   24

Definition good, excellent, fine; well

Pinyin hǎo

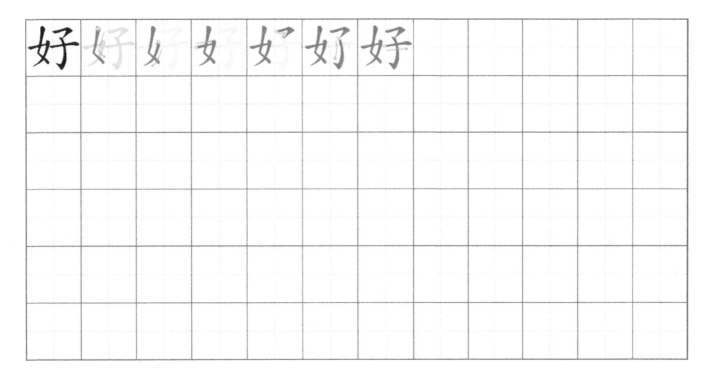

小

Definition small, tiny, insignificant

Pinyin xiǎo

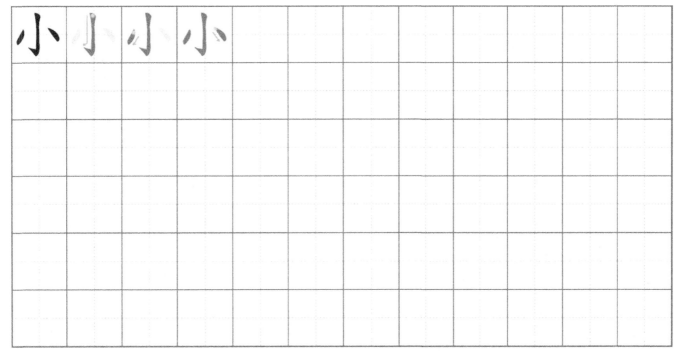

些

Definition   little, few; rather, somewhat

Pinyin   xiē

样

Definition   shape, form, pattern, style

Pinyin   yàng

Definition <u>she, her</u>

Pinyin tā

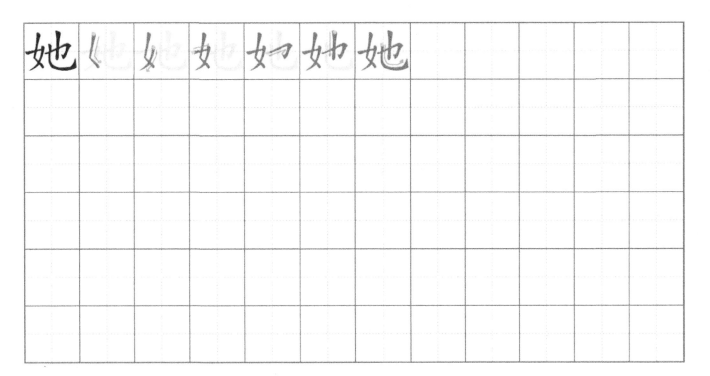

Definition <u>root, origin, source; basis</u>

Pinyin běn

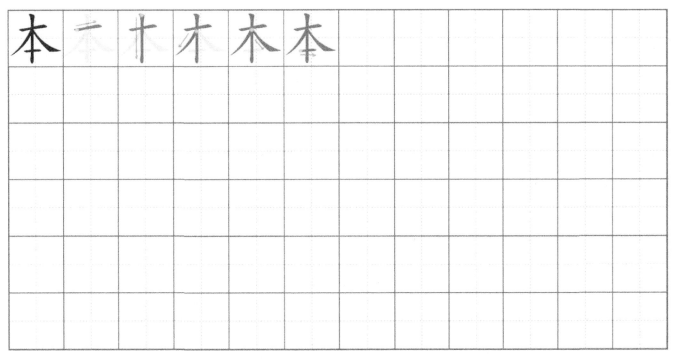

Definition in front, forward; preceding

Pinyin qián

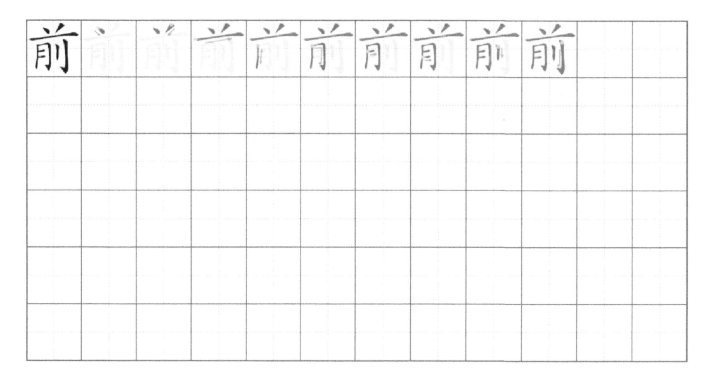

Definition open; initiate, begin, start

Pinyin kāi

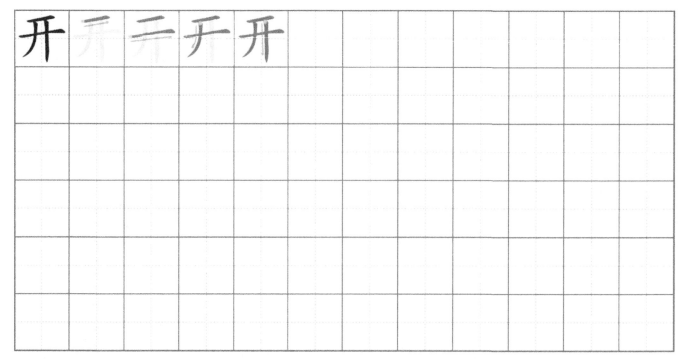

想

Definition think, speculate, plan, consider

Pinyin xiǎng

想	一想	十想	才想	木想	相	相	相	想	想	想
想	想									

机

Definition desk; machine; moment

Pinyin jī

机	机	十	才	木	机	机				

Definition <u>ten, tenth; complete; perfect</u>

Pinyin shí

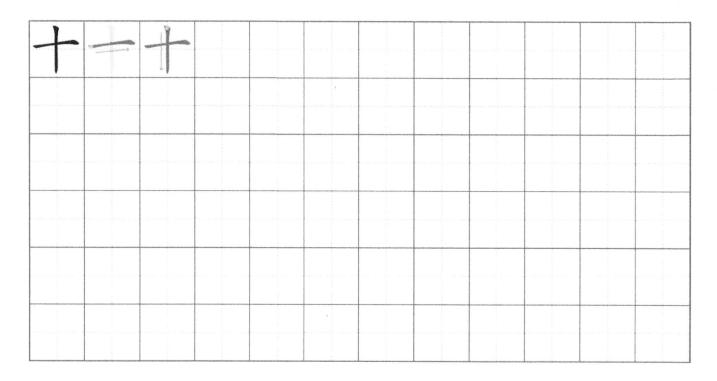

Definition <u>labor, work; worker, laborer</u>

Pinyin gōng

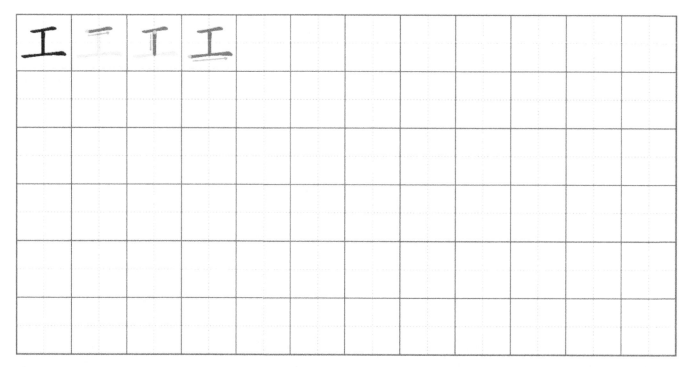

Definition bright, light, brilliant; clear

Pinyin míng

明	明	刖	日	日	明	明	明	明			

Definition three

Pinyin sān

三	三	三	三								

Definition <u>frontier pass; close; relation</u>

Pinyin guān

Definition <u>dot, speck, spot; point, degree</u>

Pinyin diǎn

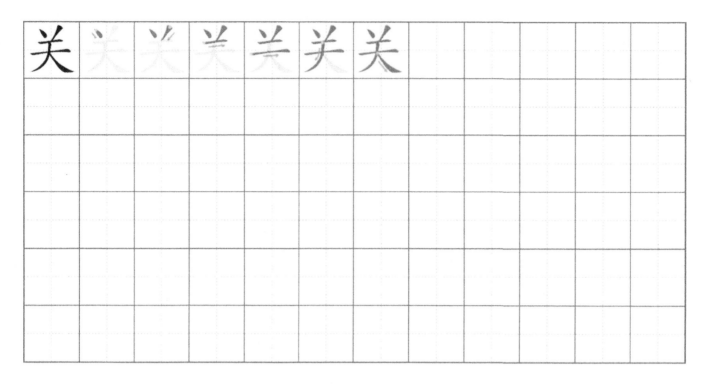

Definition <u>high, tall; lofty, elevated</u>

Pinyin gāo

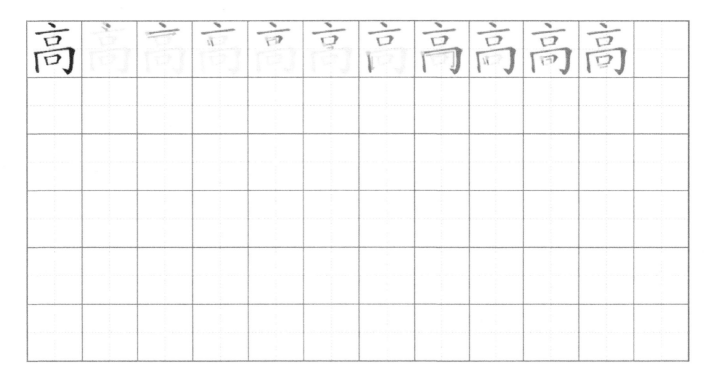

Definition <u>very, quite, much</u>

Pinyin hěn

高,很   33   HSK1 Chinese Writing Workbook

Definition <u>see, observe, behold; perceive</u>

Pinyin *jiàn*

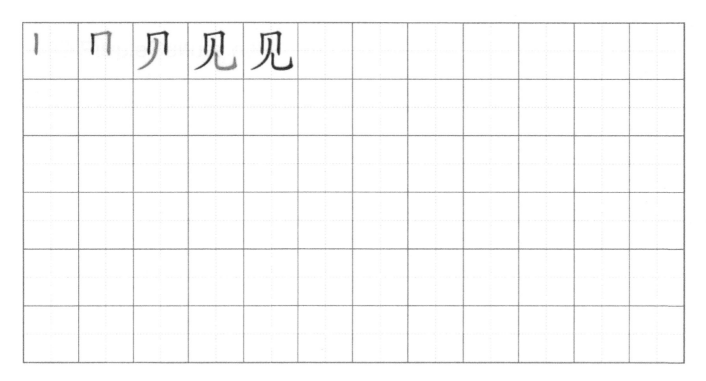

Definition <u>file of ten soldiers; mixed, miscellaneous</u>

Pinyin *shén*

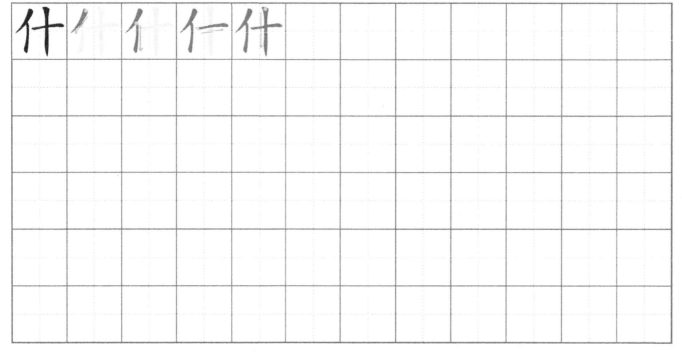

见,什   34

二

Definition <u>two; twice</u>

Pinyin èr

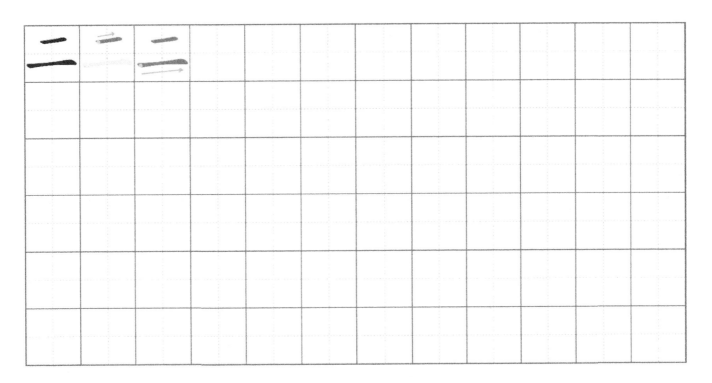

果

Definition <u>fruit; result</u>

Pinyin guǒ

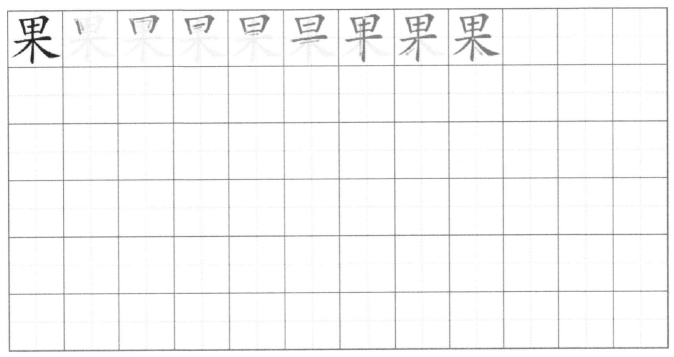

Definition   west(ern); westward, occident

Pinyin   xī

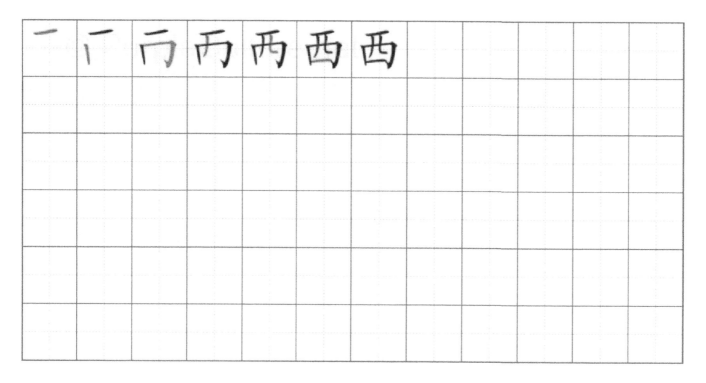

Definition   moon; month; KangXi radical 74

Pinyin   yuè

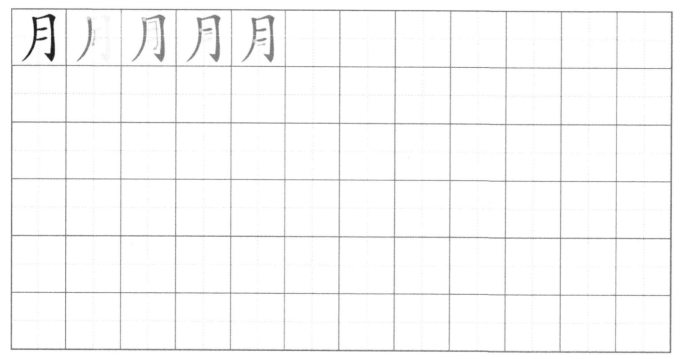

西,月   36

Definition   speech, talk, language; dialect

Pinyin   huà

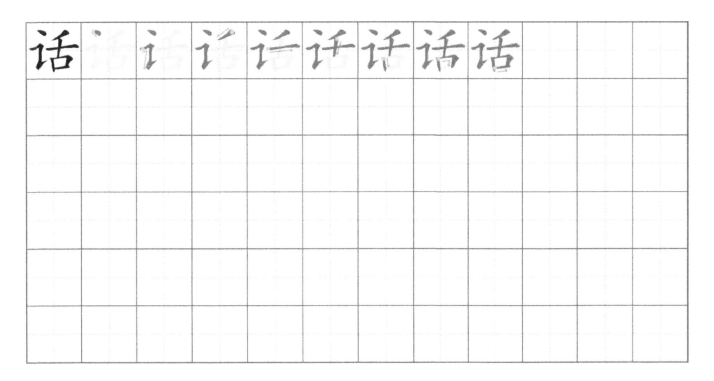

Definition   return, turn around; a time

Pinyin   huí

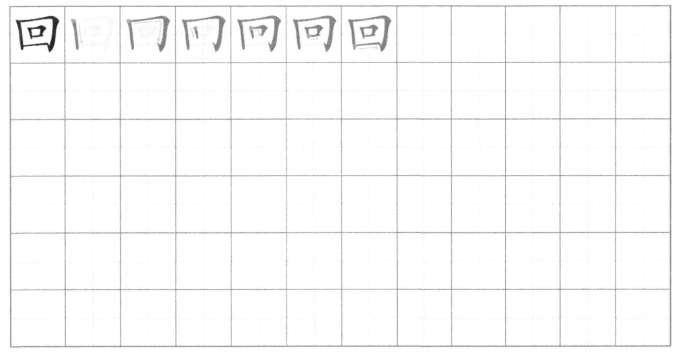

Definition <u>old, aged; experienced</u>

Pinyin lǎo

老 老 老 老 老 老 老

Definition <u>first, former, previous</u>

Pinyin xiān

先 先 先 先 先 先 先

老,先

Definition son, child; KangXi radical 10

Pinyin ér

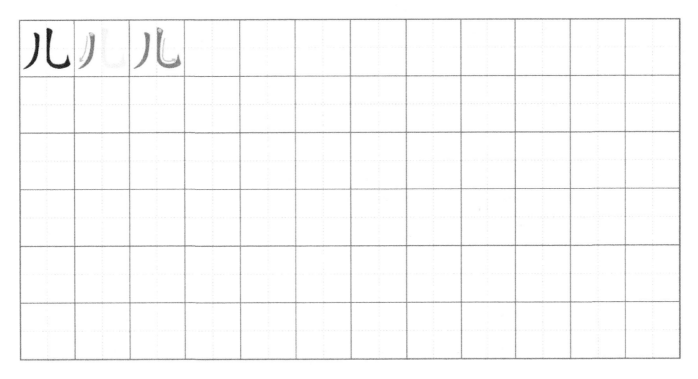

Definition east, eastern, eastward

Pinyin dōng

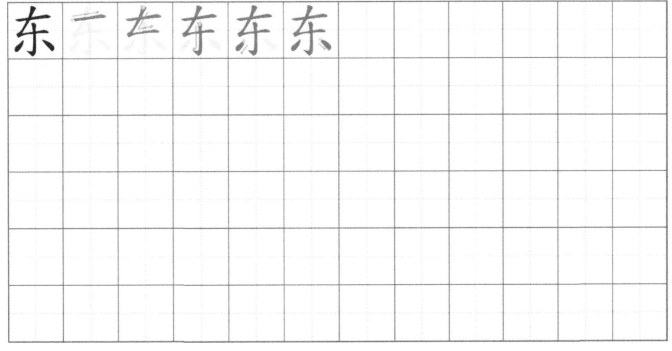

Definition water, liquid, lotion, juice

Pinyin shuǐ

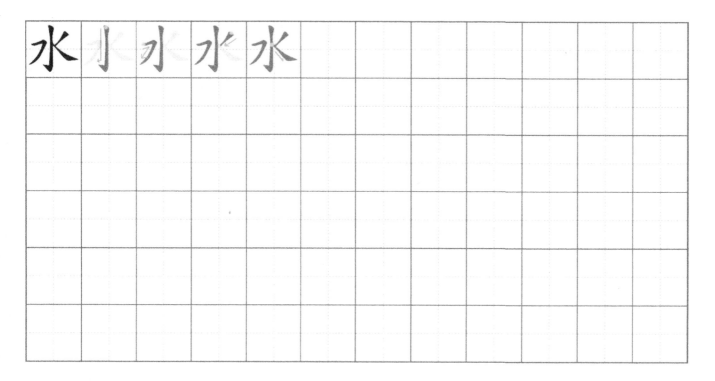

Definition name, rank, title, position

Pinyin míng

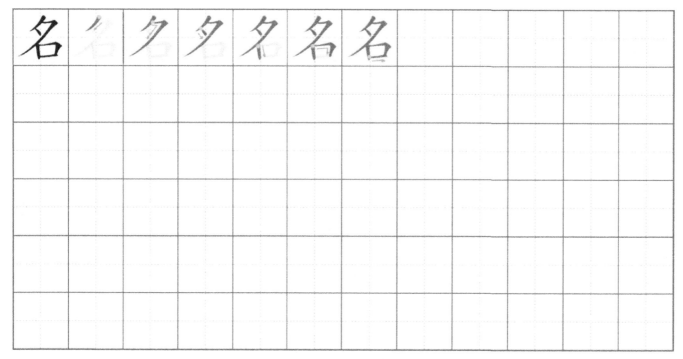

水,名

Definition <u>small table</u>

Pinyin jǐ

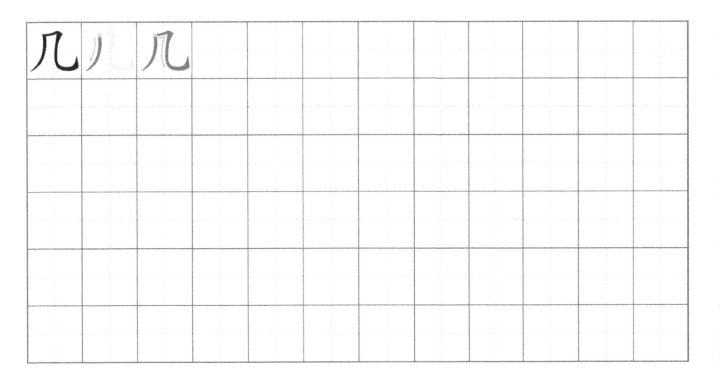

Definition <u>recognize, know, understand</u>

Pinyin rèn

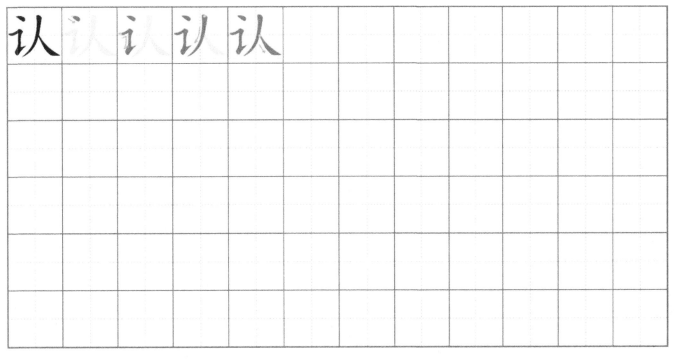

Definition <u>system; line, link, connection</u>

Pinyin xì

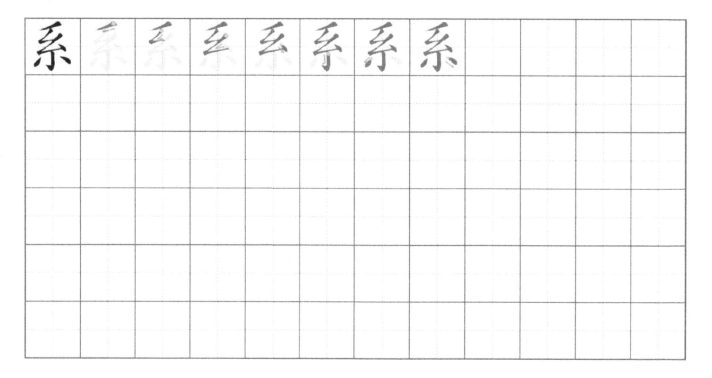

Definition <u>steam, vapor; KangXi radical 84</u>

Pinyin qì

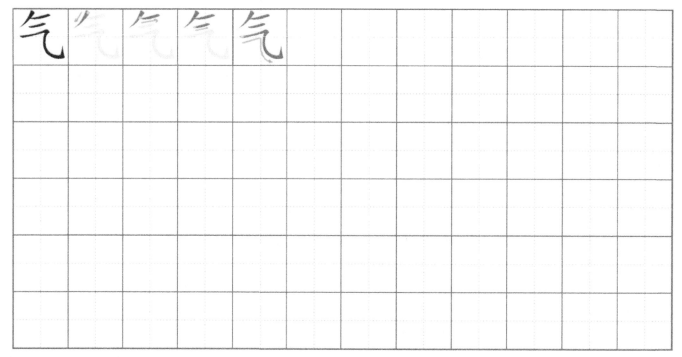

系,气

Definition strike, hit, beat; fight; attack
Pinyin dǎ

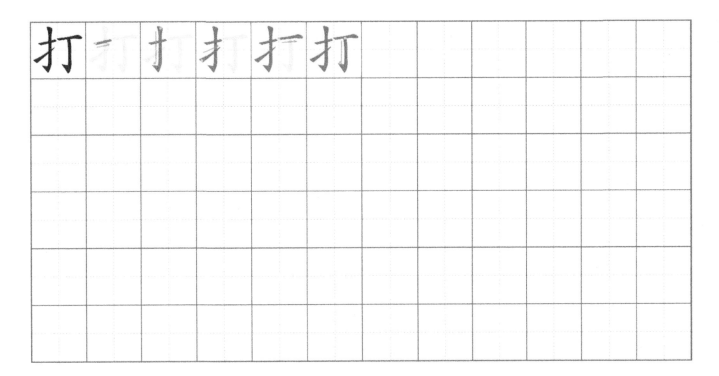

Definition woman, girl; feminine; rad. 38
Pinyin nǚ

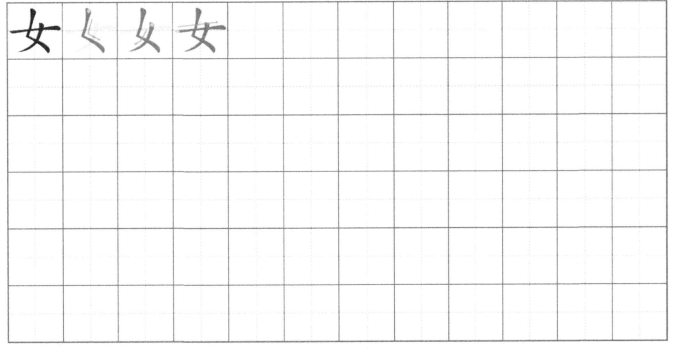

Definition <u>four</u>
Pinyin sì

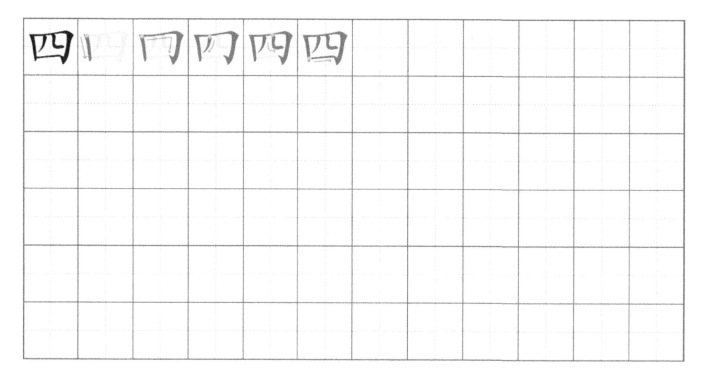

Definition <u>electricity; electric; lightning</u>
Pinyin diàn

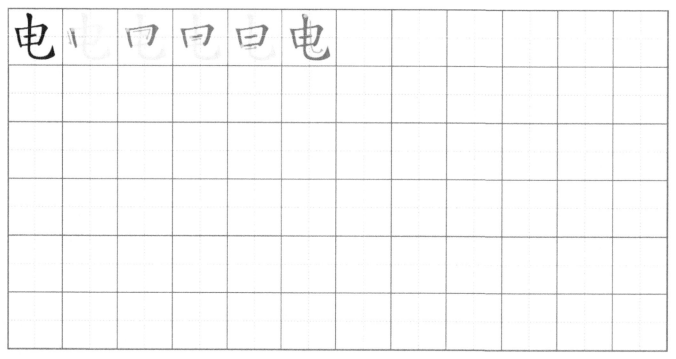

四,电

Definition <u>few, less, inadequate</u>

Pinyin shǎo

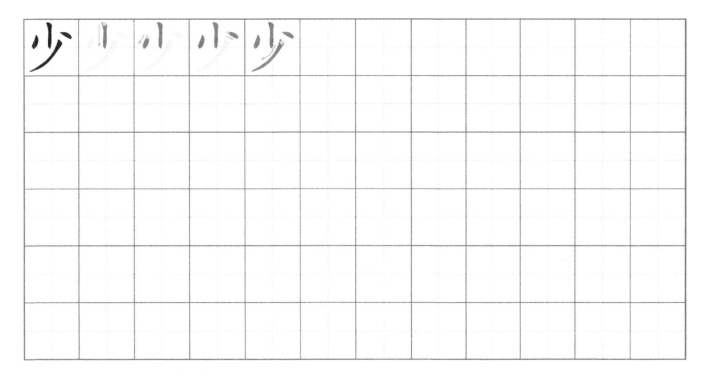

Definition <u>very, too, much; big; extreme</u>

Pinyin tài

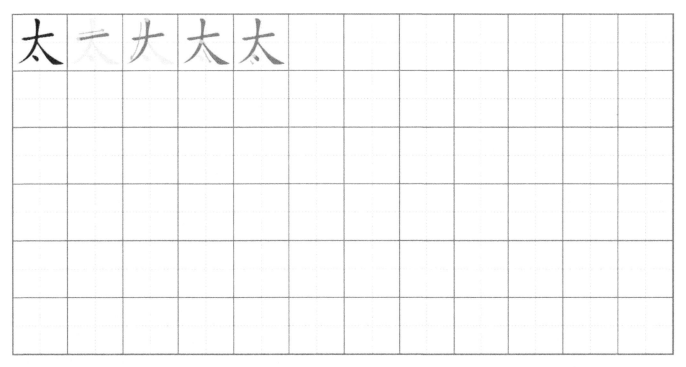

少,太   45

Definition   again, twice, re-

Pinyin   zài

Definition   work, make; act

Pinyin   zuò

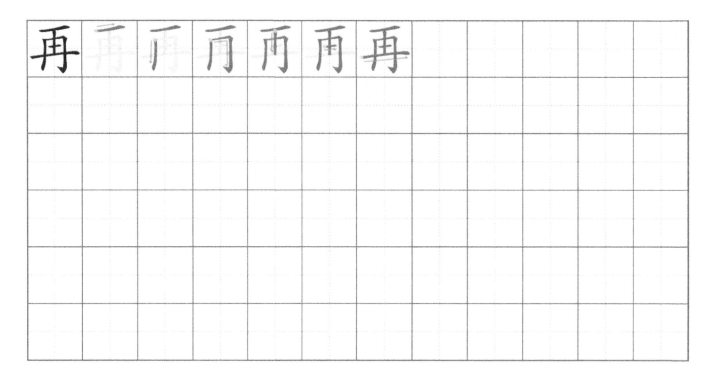

Definition period of time; date; time limit

Pinyin qī

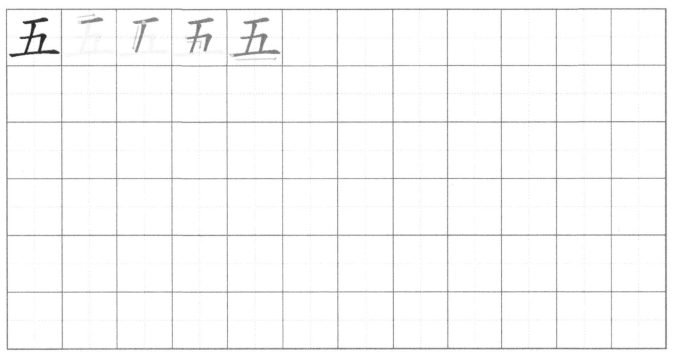

Definition five; surname

Pinyin wǔ

书

Definition book, letter, document; writings

Pinyin shū

书			书	书							

听

Definition hear; understand; obey, comply

Pinyin tīng

听							听				

Definition <u>reside, live at, dwell, lodge; stop</u>

Pinyin zhù

Definition <u>north; northern; northward</u>

Pinyin běi

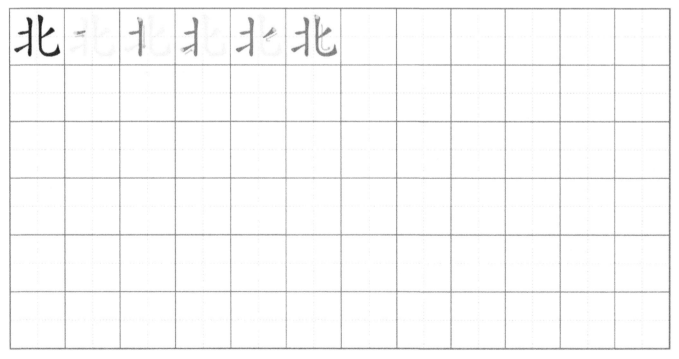

Definition to wake up from sleep; conscious

Pinyin jué

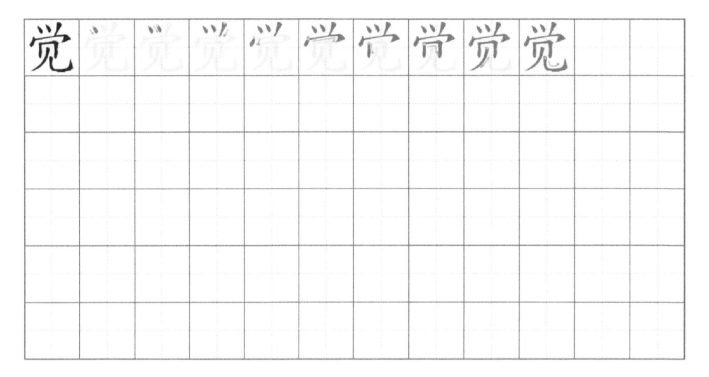

Definition teacher, master, specialist

Pinyin shī

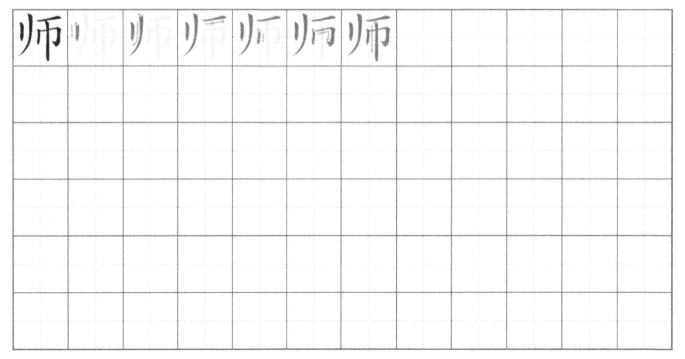

觉,师

Definition now, today, modern era

Pinyin jīn

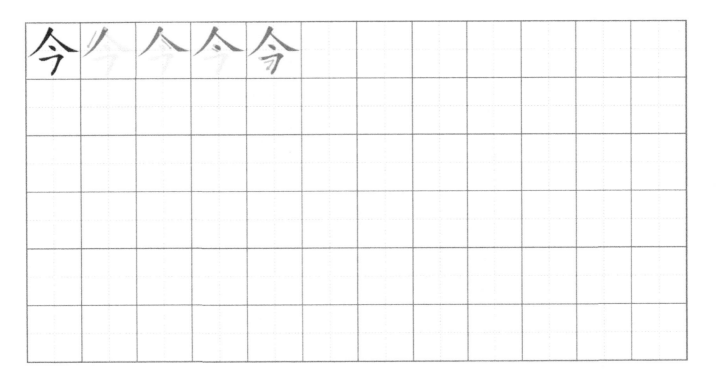

Definition courtyard, yard, court; school

Pinyin yuàn

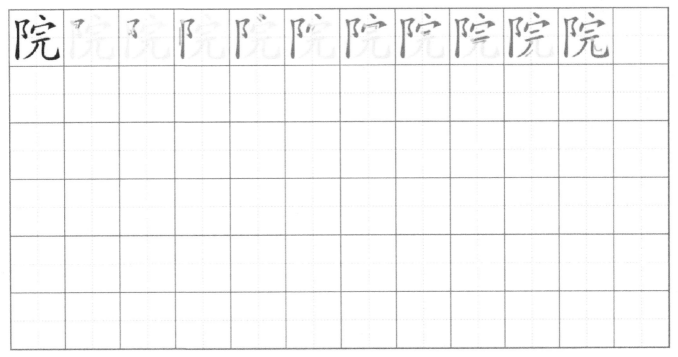

今,院   51

Definition <u>recognize, understand, know</u>

Pinyin shí

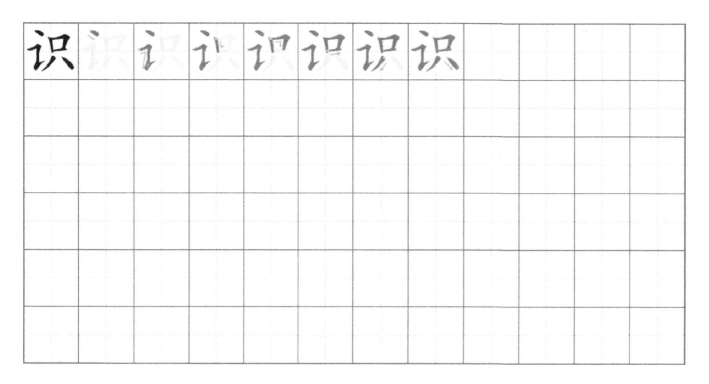

Definition <u>wait; expect; visit; greet</u>

Pinyin hòu

Definition <u>fly; go quickly; dart; high</u>

Pinyin fēi

Definition <u>cart, vehicle; carry in cart</u>

Pinyin chē

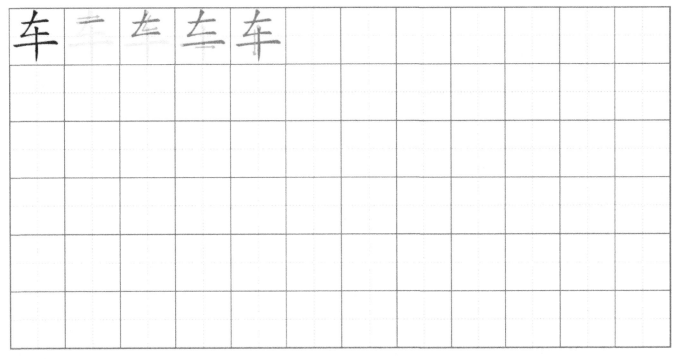

Definition   clothes; wear, dress

Pinyin   fú

服 服 服 服 服 服 服 服

Definition   what? why? how?

Pinyin   zěn

怎 怎 怎 怎 怎 怎 怎 怎 怎 怎

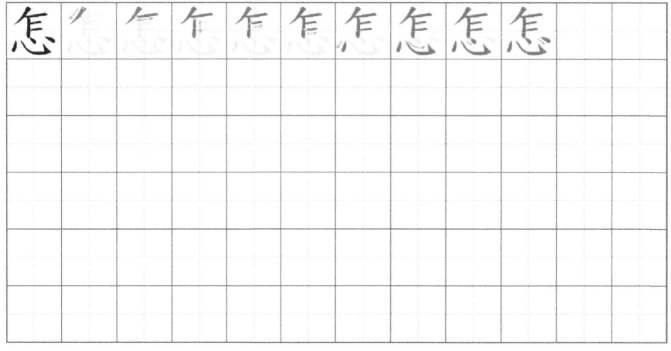

服,怎

Definition <u>interrogative or emphatic final; (Cant.) this</u>

Pinyin ne

呢	呢	呢	呢	呢	呢	呢	呢	呢			

Definition <u>cry, shout; hail, greet, call</u>

Pinyin jiào

叫	叫	叫	叫	叫	叫						

Definition   shadow; image, reflection; photograph

Pinyin   yǐng

Definition   letter, character, word

Pinyin   zì

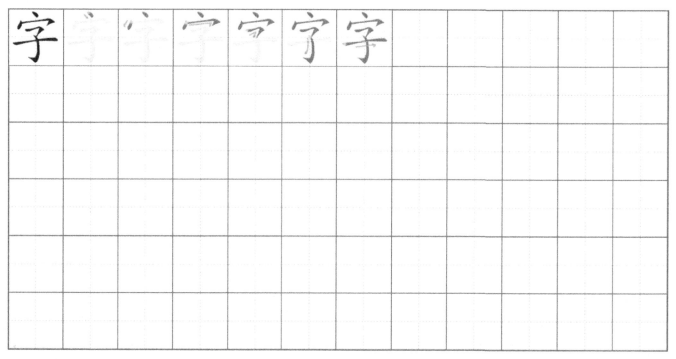

影,字

Definition <u>love, be fond of, like</u>

Pinyin ài

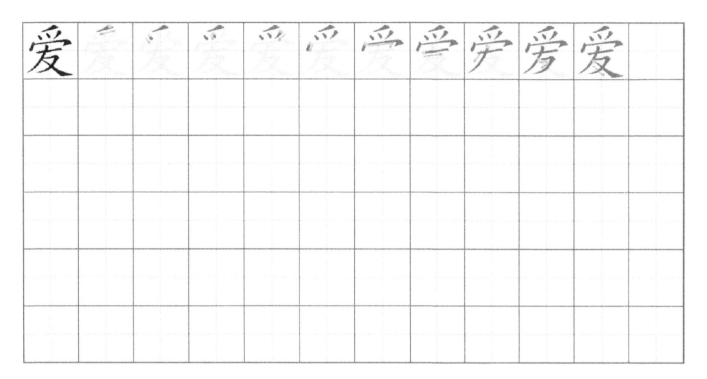

Definition <u>commerce, business, trade</u>

Pinyin shāng

Definition   ask, request; invite; please
Pinyin   qǐng

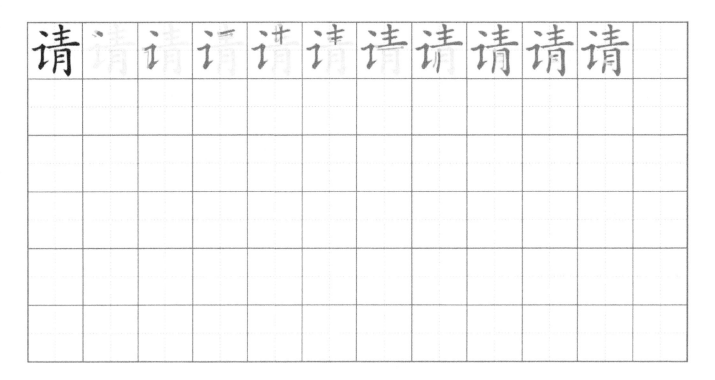

请 请 请 请 请 请 请 请 请 请

Definition   look at, inspect, observe, see
Pinyin   shì

视 视 视 视 视 视 视 视 视

请,视

Definition   nine

Pinyin   jiǔ

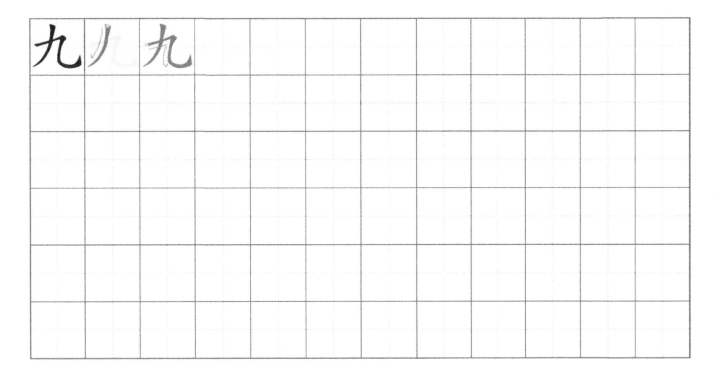

写

Definition   write; draw, sketch; compose

Pinyin   xiě

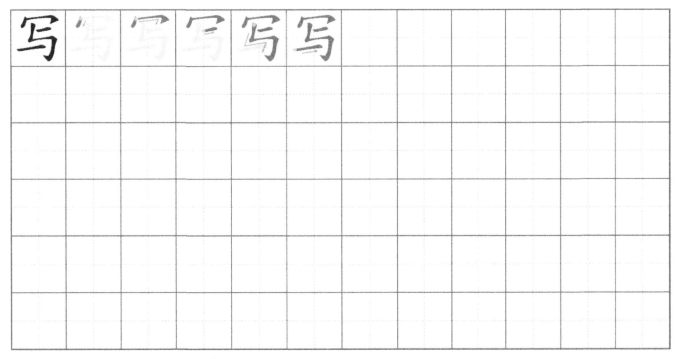

Definition <u>eight; all around, all sides</u>

Pinyin bā

Definition <u>final interrogative particle</u>

Pinyin ma

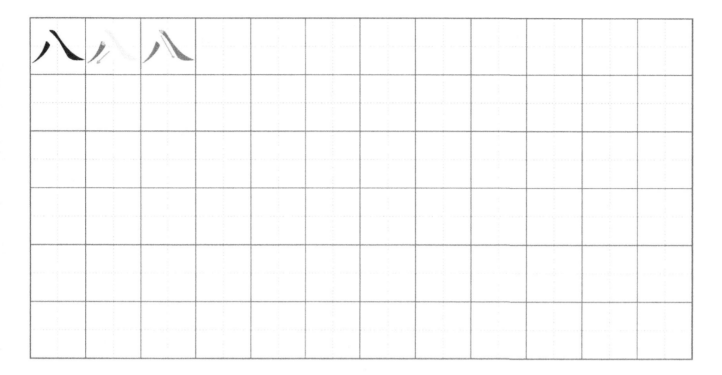

Definition eat; drink; suffer, endure, bear

Pinyin chī

Definition number six

Pinyin liù

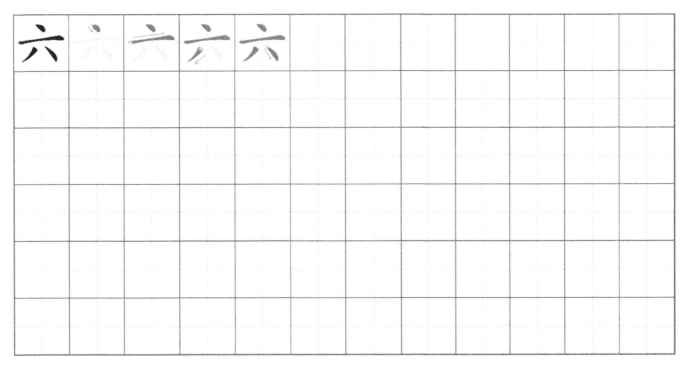

Definition <u>cure, heal; doctor, medical</u>

Pinyin yī

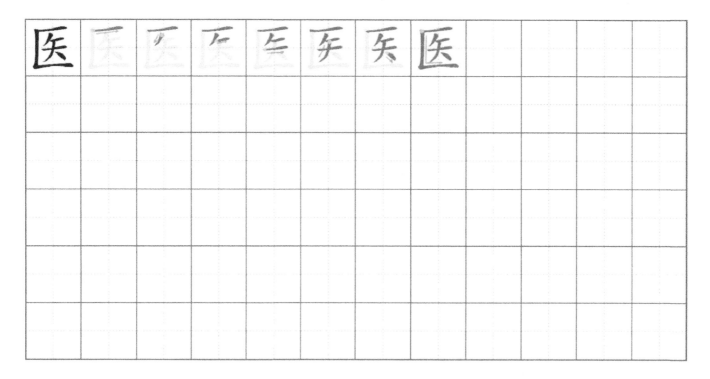

Definition <u>mark, sign; symbol; number</u>

Pinyin hào

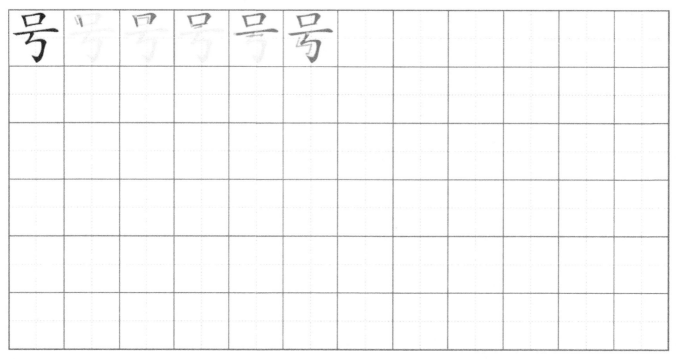

Definition <u>language, words; saying, expression</u>

Pinyin yǔ

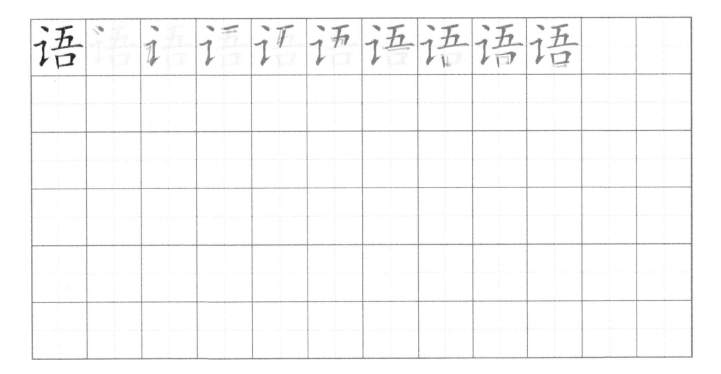

Definition <u>seven</u>

Pinyin qī

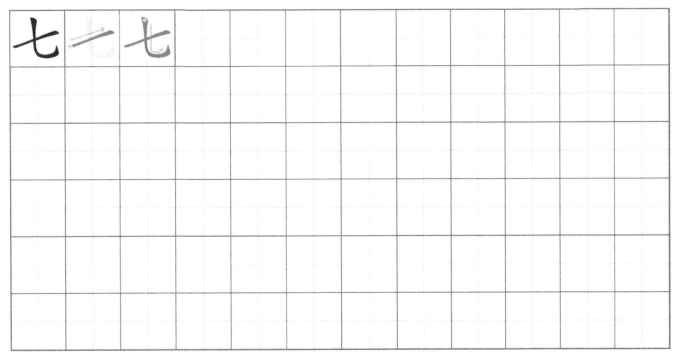

Definition thrive, prosper, flourish

Pinyin xìng

Definition a star, planet; any point of light

Pinyin xīng

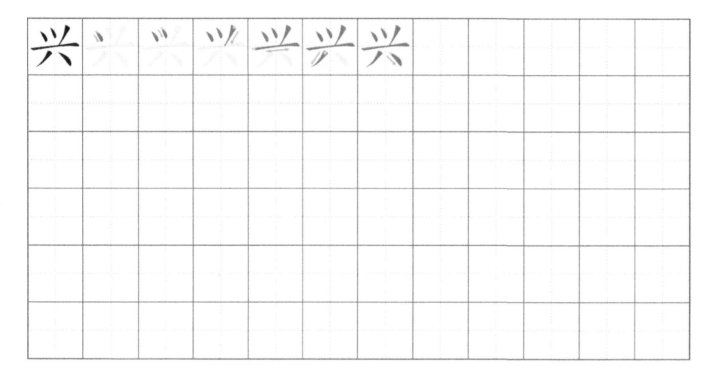

兴,星

 **Definition** <u>capital city</u>

Pinyin jīng

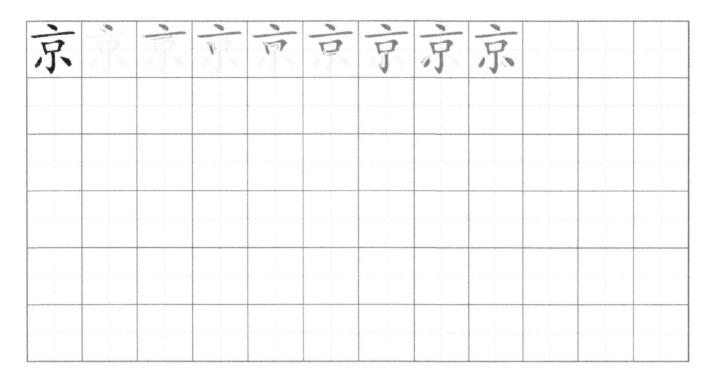

 **Definition** <u>hulled or husked uncooked rice</u>

Pinyin mǐ

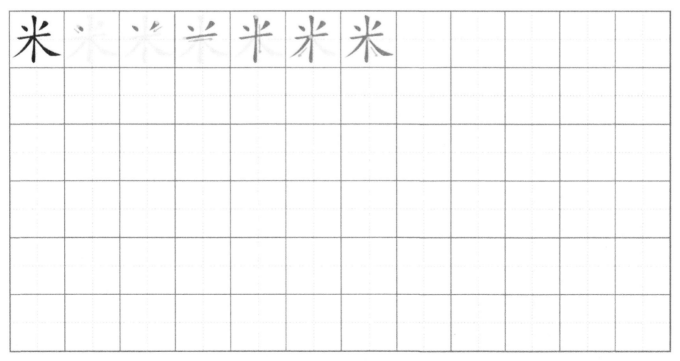

京,米   HSK1 Chinese Writing Workbook

Definition guest, traveller; customer

Pinyin kè

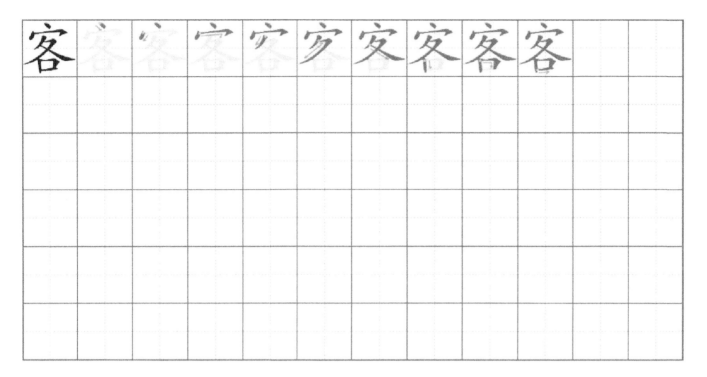

Definition friend, companion; fraternity

Pinyin yǒu

Definition money, currency, coins

Pinyin qián

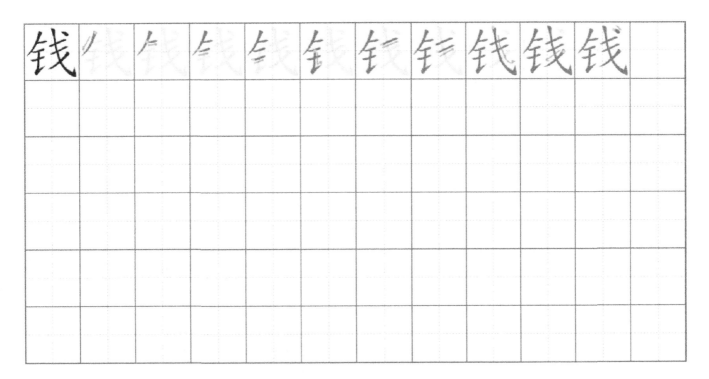

Definition hot; heat; fever; restless; zeal

Pinyin rè

Definition <u>sit; seat; ride, travel by</u>

Pinyin zuò

Definition <u>school; military field officer</u>

Pinyin xiào

Definition <u>brain</u>

Pinyin nǎo

脑	丿	几	月	月	月`	肑	肑	胶	脑	脑	

Definition <u>who? whom? whose? anyone?</u>

Pinyin shuí

谁	讠	讠	讠	讠	讠	讠	诈	谁	谁	

脑,谁   69   HSK1 Chinese Writing Workbook

Definition which? where? how?

Pinyin nǎ

哪	哪	叮	叮	叨	呀	呀	哪	哪	哪	哪

Definition like, love, enjoy; joyful thing

Pinyin xǐ

喜喜	一	十	士	吉	吉	吉	吉	吉	壴	壴	喜

哪,喜

Definition <u>practice; flapping wings</u>

Pinyin xí

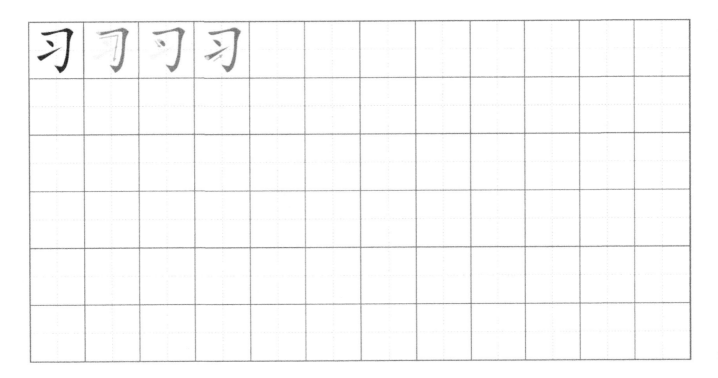

Definition <u>happy, pleased, glad; joy; enjoy</u>

Pinyin huān

Definition <u>cold, cool; lonely</u>

Pinyin lěng

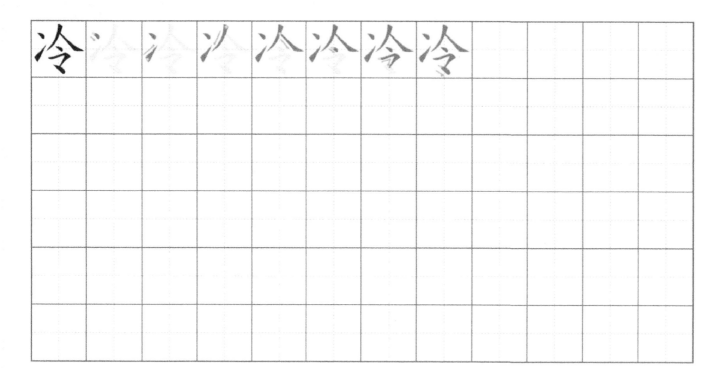

Definition <u>Chinese people; Chinese language</u>

Pinyin hàn

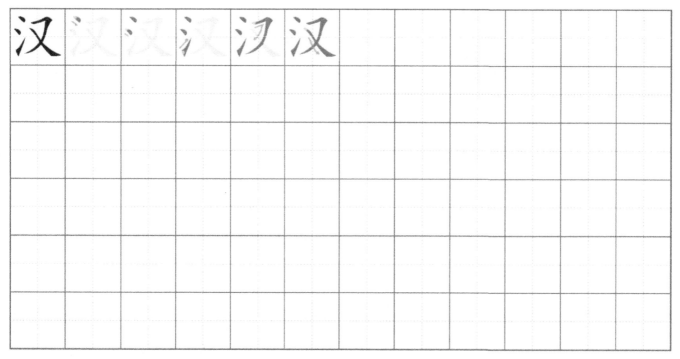

冷,汉

Definition clothes, clothing; cover, skin

Pinyin yī

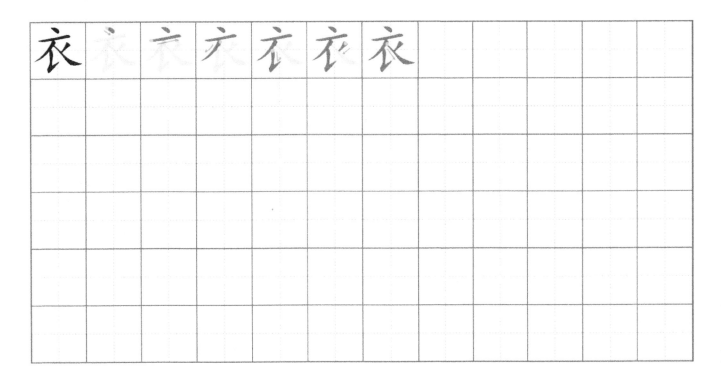

Definition mother, mama

Pinyin mā

Definition   read, study; pronounce

Pinyin   dú

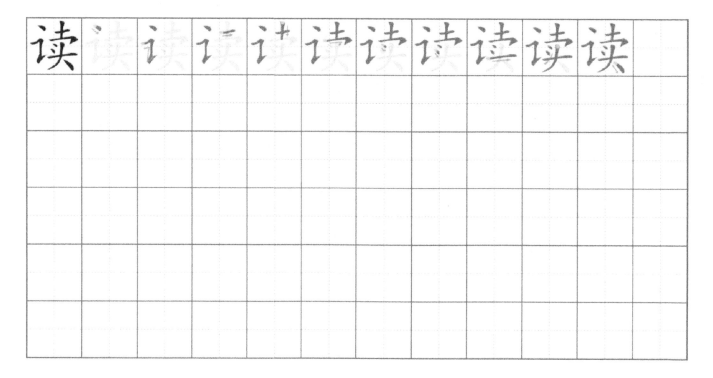

Definition   buy, purchase; bribe, persuade

Pinyin   mǎi

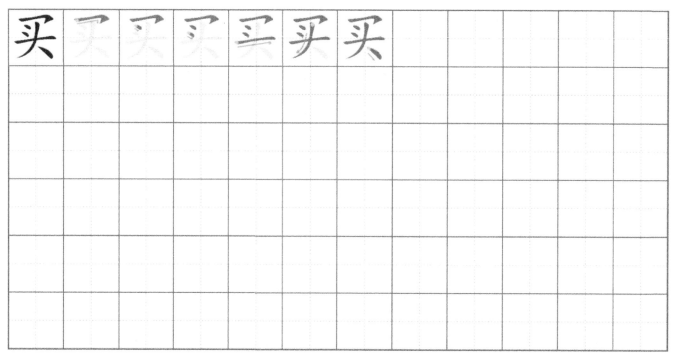

读,买

Definition   year; age; harvest

Pinyin   suì

岁 岁 岁 岁 岁 岁 岁

Definition   piece, lump; dollar

Pinyin   kuài

块 块 块 块 块 块 块

姐

Definition <u>elder sister, young lady</u>

Pinyin jiě

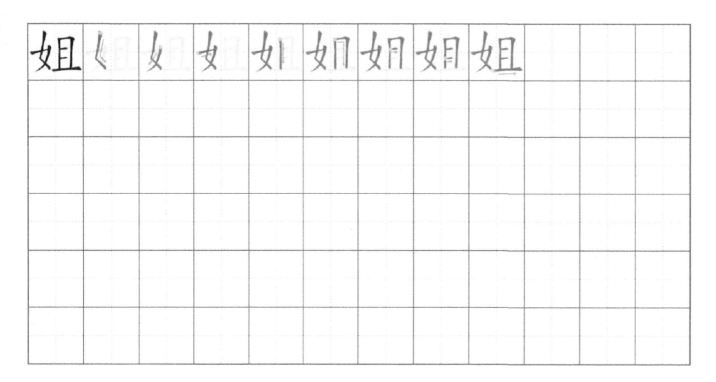

亮

Definition <u>bright, brilliant, radiant, light</u>

Pinyin liàng

Definition friend, pal, acquaintance
Pinyin péng

朋	刀	刀	月	月	朋	朋	朋	朋		

Definition thank; decline
Pinyin xiè

谢	讠	讠	讠	讠	讠	讠	讠	讠	谢	谢
谢										

Definition <u>clock; bell</u>

Pinyin zhōng

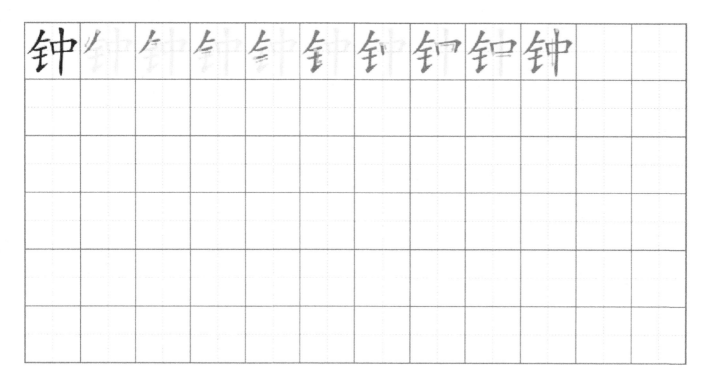

Definition <u>rain; rainy; KangXi radical 173</u>

Pinyin yǔ

钟,雨

饭

Definition <u>cooked rice; food, meal</u>

Pinyin fàn

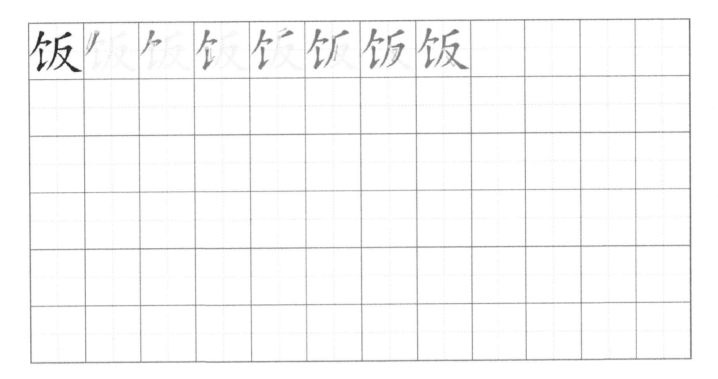

睡

Definition <u>sleep, doze</u>

Pinyin shuì

Definition <u>drink; shout, call out</u>

Pinyin hē

喝	喝	喝	喝	喝	喝	喝	喝	喝	喝	喝
喝										

午

Definition <u>noon; 7th terrestrial branch</u>

Pinyin wǔ

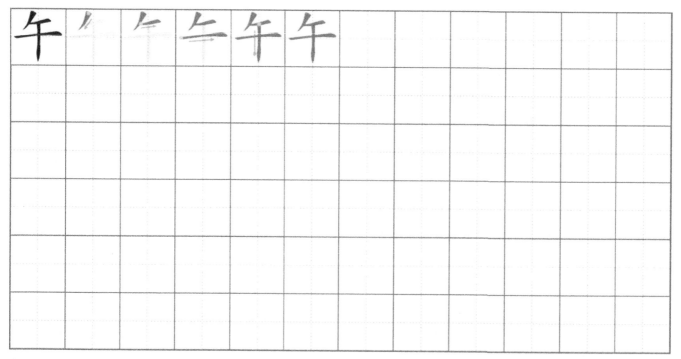

Definition <u>shop, store; inn, hotel</u>

Pinyin diàn

Definition <u>father, papa</u>

Pinyin bà

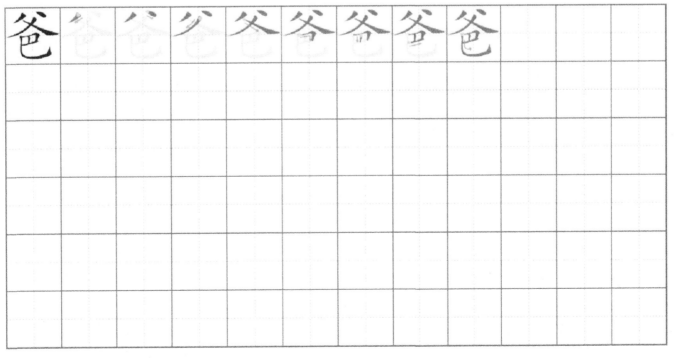

Definition <u>table, desk, stand</u>

Pinyin zhuō

桌	桌	桌	桌	卓	桌	桌	卓	桌	桌	桌	

Definition <u>vegetables; dish, order; food</u>

Pinyin cài

菜	菜	菜	菜	菜	菜	菜	菜	菜	菜	菜	

桌,菜

Definition <u>tea</u>

Pinyin chá

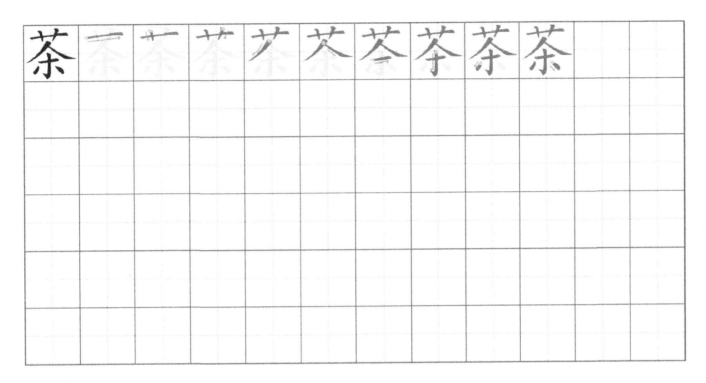

Definition <u>dog, canis familiaris</u>

Pinyin gǒu

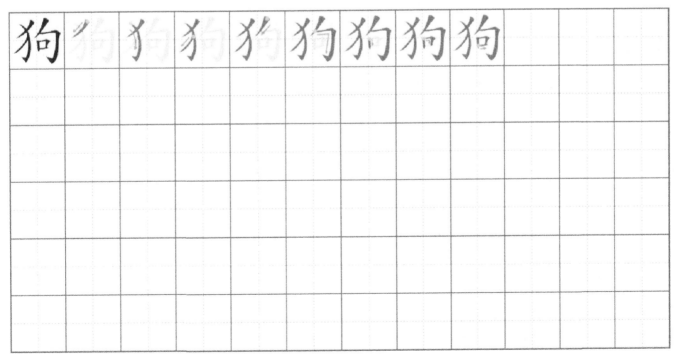

茶,狗

83

HSK1 Chinese Writing Workbook

Definition cup, glass

Pinyin bēi

Definition rent, lease; rental; tax

Pinyin zū

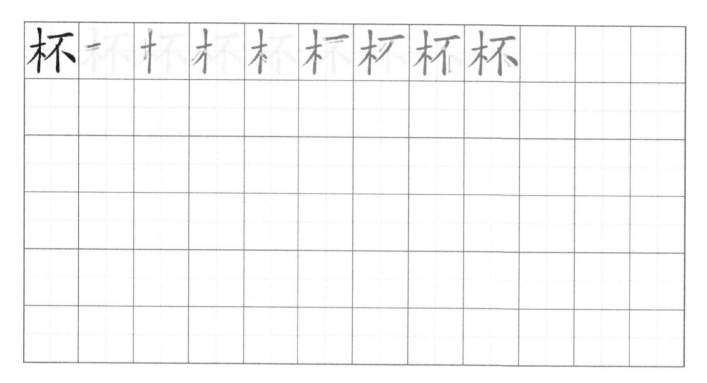

Definition yesterday; in former times, past

Pinyin zuó

昨	丨	刀	日	日	日	昨	昨	昨		

Definition float, drift; tossed about

Pinyin piào

漂	漂	漂	漂	漂	漂	漂	漂	漂	漂
漂	漂	漂							

Definition <u>chair, seat</u>
Pinyin yǐ

一	十	才	才	术	杧	栌	栌	栌	梼	梼	椅
椅											

猫

Definition <u>cat</u>
Pinyin māo

猫	猫	猫	猫	猫	猫	猫	猫	猫	猫	猫

椅,猫

Definition <u>interjection to call attention</u>

Pinyin wèi

丶	口	口	叫	叩	吗	呷	喂	喂	喂	喂	喂
喂											

Definition <u>artemisia; duckweed; apple</u>

Pinyin píng

苹	苹	苹	苹	苹	苹	苹	苹	苹			

(wǒ) I, me

我

(wǒmen) we, us

我们

(nǐ) you

你

(nǐmen) you (pl.)

你们

(tā) he, him

他

(tā) she, her

她

(tāmen) they

他们

(tāmen) they (females, pl.)

她们

(zhè) this

这

(zhèr) here

这儿

(nà) that

那

(nàr) there

那儿

(nǎ) how, which

哪

(nǎr) where

哪儿

(shuí) who

谁

(shén me) what, why

什么

(duōshǎo) how many, how much

多少

(jǐ) a few, how many

几

(zěnme) how

怎么

(zěnmeyàng) how about

怎么样

(yī) one

一

(èr) two

二

(sān) three

三

(sì) four

四

(wǔ) five

五

(liù) six

六

(qī) seven

七

(bā) eight

八

(jiǔ) nine

九

(shí) ten

十

Compound words practice

(líng) zero

零

(gè) a, an

个

(suì) year

岁

(běn) volume

本

(xiē) some

些

(kuài) piece

块

(bù) no

不

(méi) no

没

(hěn) quite, very

很

(tài) too

太

(dōu) all

都

(hé) and

和

(zài) in, at

在

(de) (possessive particle)

的

(le) (completed action particle)

了

(ma) (question particle)

吗

(ne) (reciprocal particle)

呢

(wèi) hello

喂

(jiā) home

家

(xuéxiào) school

学校

Compound words practice

92

(fàndiàn) restaurant

饭店

(shāngdiàn) store

商店

(yīyuàn) hospital

医院

(huǒchēzhàn) train station

火车站

(zhōng guó) China

中国

(běijīng) Beijing

北京

(shàng) up

上

(xià) down

下

(qiánmiàn) front

前面

(hòumiàn) behind

后面

(lǐmiàn) inside

里

(jīntiān) today

今天

(míngtiān) tomorrow

明天

(zuótiān) yesterday

昨天

(shàngwǔ) morning

上午

(zhōngwǔ) noon

中午

(xiàwǔ) afternoon

下午

(nián) year

年

(yuè) month

月

(rì) day

日

(xīngqī) week

星 期

(diǎn) dot, spot

点

(fēnzhōng) minute

分 钟

(xiànzài) now

现 在

(shíhou) time

时 候

(bàba) father

爸 爸

(māma) mother

妈 妈

(érzi) son

儿 子

(nǚér) daughter

女 儿

(lǎoshī) teacher

老 师

(xuéshēng) student

学生

(tóngxué) classmate

同学

(péngyou) friend

朋友

(yīshēng) doctor

医生

(xiānsheng) sir

先生

(xiǎojiě) Miss

小姐

(yīfu) cloth

衣服

(shuǐ) water

水

(cài) vegetable

菜

(mǐfàn) rice

米饭

(shuǐguǒ) fruit

水 果

(píngguǒ) apple

苹 果

(chá) tea

茶

(bēizi) cup

杯 子

(qián) money

钱

(fēijī) airplane

飞 机

(chūzūchē) taxi

出 租 车

(diànshì) television

电 视

(diànnǎo) computer

电 脑

(diànyǐng) movie

电 影

(tiānqì) weather

天气

(māo) cat

猫

(gǒu) dog

狗

(dōngxi) thing

东西

(rén) person

人

(míngzi) name

名字

(shū) book

书

(hànyǔ) Chinese

汉语

(zì) character

字

(zhuōzi) desk

桌子

(yǐzi) chair

椅 子

(xièxie) thank

谢 谢

(búkèqì) you are welcome

不 客 气

(zàijiàn) good-bye

再 见

(qǐng) please

请

(duìbùqǐ) sorry

对 不 起

(méiguānxì) It doesn't matter

没 关 系

(shì) be (am, is, are)

是

(yǒu) have

有

(kàn) look

看

(tīng) listen

听

(shuōhuà) speak

说话

(dú) read

读

(xiě) write

写

(kànjiàn) see

看见

(jiào) call

叫

(lái) come

来

(huí) return

回

(qù) go

去

(chī) eat

吃

Compound words practice

100

(hē) drink

喝

(shuìjiào) sleep

睡 觉

(dǎdiànhuà) call up

打 电 话

(zuò) do

做

(mǎi) buy

买

(kāi) open

开

(zuò) sit

坐

(zhù) live

住

(xuéxí) study

学 习

(gōngzuò) work

工 作

(xiàyǔ) rain

下雨

(ài) love

爱

(xǐhuān) love, like

喜欢

(xiǎng) want

想

(rènshi) know

认识

(huì) can

会

(néng) can, be able to

能

(hǎo) good

好

(dà) big

大

(xiǎo) small

小

(duō) many, much

多

(shǎo) few, little

少

(lěng) cold

冷

(rè) hot

热

(gāoxìng) happy

高兴

(piàoliàng) beautiful

漂亮

(Zhège píngguǒ yīkuài qián.) This apple costs one yuan.

这个苹果一块钱。

(Tā shì wǒmen de hǎo péngyǒu.) She is our good friend.

她是我们的好朋友。

(Wǒ hěn xǐhuan zhè běn shū) I like this book very much.

我 很 喜 欢 这 本 书。

(Zhè shì wǒ mǎi de zhuōzi hé yǐzi) I bought this table and chair.

这 是 我 买 的 桌 子 和 椅 子。

(Nǐ hē shuǐ ma?) Do you want water?

你 喝 水 吗？

(Shéi huì shuō Hànyǔ?) Who can speak Chinese?

谁 会 说 汉 语？

(Zuótiān shàngwǔ tiānqì zěnmeyàng?) How was the weather yesterday morning?

昨 天 上 午 天 气 怎 么 样？

Compound words practice

的	一
是	不
了	在
人	有
我	他

one; a, an; alone

Pinyin

yī

possessive, adjectival suffix

Pinyin

de

no, not; un-; negative prefix

Pinyin

bù

indeed, yes, right; to be; demonstrative pronoun, this, that

Pinyin

shì

be at, in, on; consist in, rest

Pinyin

zài

to finish; particle of completed action

Pinyin

le

have, own, possess; exist

Pinyin

yǒu

man; people; mankind; someone else

Pinyin

rén

other, another; he, she, it

Pinyin

tā

our, us, i, me, my, we

Pinyin

wǒ

这	个
们	中
来	上
大	和
国	说

numerary adjunct, piece; single

Pinyin

gè

this, the, here

Pinyin

zhè

central; center, middle; in the midst of; hit (target); attain

Pinyin

zhōng

adjunct pronoun indicate plural

Pinyin

men

top; superior, highest; go up, send up

Pinyin

shàng

come, coming; return, returning

Pinyin

lái

harmony, peace; peaceful, calm

Pinyin

hé

big, great, vast, large, high

Pinyin

dà

speak, say, talk; scold, upbraid

Pinyin

shuō

nation, country, nation-state

Pinyin

guó

出	时
你	会
生	对
子	能
下	那

go out, send out; stand; produce

Pinyin

chū

time, season; era, age, period

Pinyin

shí

you, second person pronoun

Pinyin

nǐ

assemble, meet together; meeting

Pinyin

huì

life, living, lifetime; birth

Pinyin

shēng

correct, right; facing, opposed

Pinyin

duì

offspring, child; fruit, seed of; 1st terrestrial branch

Pinyin

zi

to be able; can, permitted to; ability

Pinyin

néng

under, underneath, below; down; inferior; bring down

Pinyin

xià

that, that one, those

Pinyin

nà

年	后
作	里
家	多
么	去
学	都

queen, empress, sovereign; (simp. for 後) behind, rear, after

Pinyin

hòu

year

Pinyin

nián

unit of distance; village; lane

Pinyin

lǐ

make; work; compose, write; act, perform

Pinyin

zuò

much, many; more than, over

Pinyin

duō

house, home, residence; family

Pinyin

jiā

go away, leave, depart

Pinyin

qù

interrogative particle; repetition of a tune small; tender

Pinyin

me

metropolis, capital; all, the whole; elegant, refined

Pinyin

dōu

learning, knowledge; school

Pinyin

xué

现	同
面	没
看	起
分	天
小	好

appear, manifest, become visible

Pinyin

xiàn

same, similar; together with

Pinyin

tóng

face; surface; plane; side, dimension

Pinyin

miàn

not, have not, none; drown, sink

Pinyin

méi

look, see; examine, scrutinize

Pinyin

kàn

rise, stand up; go up; begin

Pinyin

qǐ

divide; small unit of time etc.

Pinyin

fēn

sky, heaven; god, celestial

Pinyin

tiān

small, tiny, insignificant

Pinyin

xiǎo

good, excellent, fine; well

Pinyin

hǎo

样 些

本 她

开 前

机 想

工 十

shape, form, pattern, style

Pinyin

yàng

little, few; rather, somewhat

Pinyin

xiē

root, origin, source; basis

Pinyin

běn

she, her

Pinyin

tā

open; initiate, begin, start

Pinyin

kāi

in front, forward; preceding

Pinyin

qián

desk; machine; moment

Pinyin

jī

think, speculate, plan, consider

Pinyin

xiǎng

labor, work; worker, laborer

Pinyin

gōng

ten, tenth; complete; perfect

Pinyin

shí

明 三
关 点
高 很
见 什
二 果

three

Pinyin

sān

bright, light, brilliant; clear

Pinyin

míng

dot, speck, spot; point, degree

Pinyin

diǎn

frontier pass; close; relation

Pinyin

guān

very, quite, much

Pinyin

hěn

high, tall; lofty, elevated

Pinyin

gāo

file of ten soldiers; mixed, miscellaneous

Pinyin

shén

see, observe, behold; perceive

Pinyin

jiàn

fruit; result

Pinyin

guǒ

two; twice

Pinyin

èr

西	月
话	回
老	先
儿	东
水	名

moon; month; KangXi radical 74

Pinyin

yuè

west(ern); westward, occident

Pinyin

xī

return, turn around; a time

Pinyin

huí

speech, talk, language; dialect

Pinyin

huà

first, former, previous

Pinyin

xiān

old, aged; experienced

Pinyin

lǎo

east, eastern, eastward

Pinyin

dōng

son, child; KangXi radical 10

Pinyin

ér

name, rank, title, position

Pinyin

míng

water, liquid, lotion, juice

Pinyin

shuǐ

几

系

打

四

少

认

气

女

电

太

recognize, know, understand

Pinyin

rèn

small table

Pinyin

jǐ

steam, vapor; KangXi radical 84

Pinyin

qì

system; line, link, connection

Pinyin

xì

woman, girl; feminine; rad. 38

Pinyin

nǚ

strike, hit, beat; fight; attack

Pinyin

dǎ

electricity; electric; lightning

Pinyin

diàn

four

Pinyin

sì

very, too, much; big; extreme

Pinyin

tài

few, less, inadequate

Pinyin

shǎo

做	再
五	期
听	书
北	住
师	觉

work, make; act

Pinyin

zuò

again, twice, re-

Pinyin

zài

five; surname

Pinyin

wǔ

period of time; date; time limit

Pinyin

qī

hear; understand; obey, comply

Pinyin

tīng

book, letter, document; writings

Pinyin

shū

north; northern; northward

Pinyin

běi

reside, live at, dwell, lodge; stop

Pinyin

zhù

teacher, master, specialist

Pinyin

shī

to wake up from sleep; conscious

Pinyin

jué

今
识
飞
服
呢

院
候
车
怎
叫

courtyard, yard, court; school

Pinyin

yuàn

now, today, modern era

Pinyin

jīn

wait; expect; visit; greet

Pinyin

hòu

recognize, understand, know

Pinyin

shí

cart, vehicle; carry in cart

Pinyin

chē

fly; go quickly; dart; high

Pinyin

fēi

what? why? how?

Pinyin

zěn

clothes; wear, dress

Pinyin

fú

cry, shout; hail, greet, call

Pinyin

jiào

interrogative or emphatic final; (Cant.) this

Pinyin

ne

影	字
爱	商
请	视
九	写
八	吗

letter, character, word

Pinyin

zì

shadow; image, reflection; photograph

Pinyin

yǐng

commerce, business, trade

Pinyin

shāng

love, be fond of, like

Pinyin

ài

look at, inspect, observe, see

Pinyin

shì

ask, request; invite; please

Pinyin

qǐng

write; draw, sketch; compose

Pinyin

xiě

nine

Pinyin

jiǔ

final interrogative particle

Pinyin

ma

eight; all around, all sides

Pinyin

bā

吃	六
医	号
语	七
兴	星
京	米

number six

Pinyin
liù

eat; drink; suffer, endure, bear

Pinyin
chī

mark, sign; symbol; number

Pinyin
hào

cure, heal; doctor, medical

Pinyin
yī

seven

Pinyin
qī

language, words; saying, expression

Pinyin
yǔ

a star, planet; any point of light

Pinyin
xīng

thrive, prosper, flourish

Pinyin
xìng

hulled or husked uncooked rice

Pinyin
mǐ

capital city

Pinyin
jīng

客	友
钱	热
坐	校
脑	谁
哪	喜

friend, companion; fraternity

Pinyin

yǒu

guest, traveller; customer

Pinyin

kè

hot; heat; fever; restless; zeal

Pinyin

rè

money, currency, coins

Pinyin

qián

school; military field officer

Pinyin

xiào

sit; seat; ride, travel by

Pinyin

zuò

who? whom? whose? anyone?

Pinyin

shuí

brain

Pinyin

nǎo

like, love, enjoy; joyful thing

Pinyin

xǐ

which? where? how?

Pinyin

nǎ

习	欢
冷	汉
衣	妈
读	买
岁	块

happy, pleased, glad; joy; enjoy

Pinyin

huān

practice; flapping wings

Pinyin

xí

Chinese people; Chinese language

Pinyin

hàn

cold, cool; lonely

Pinyin

lěng

mother, mama

Pinyin

mā

clothes, clothing; cover, skin

Pinyin

yī

buy, purchase; bribe, persuade

Pinyin

mǎi

read, study; pronounce

Pinyin

dú

piece, lump; dollar

Pinyin

kuài

year; age; harvest

Pinyin

suì

姐	亮
朋	谢
钟	雨
饭	睡
喝	午

bright, brilliant, radiant, light

Pinyin

liàng

elder sister, young lady

Pinyin

jiě

thank; decline

Pinyin

xiè

friend, pal, acquaintance

Pinyin

péng

rain; rainy; KangXi radical 173

Pinyin

yǔ

clock; bell

Pinyin

zhōng

sleep, doze

Pinyin

shuì

cooked rice; food, meal

Pinyin

fàn

noon; 7th terrestrial branch

Pinyin

wǔ

drink; shout, call out

Pinyin

hē

店

桌

茶

杯

昨

爸

菜

狗

租

漂

father, papa

Pinyin
bà

shop, store; inn, hotel

Pinyin
diàn

vegetables; dish, order; food

Pinyin
cài

table, desk, stand

Pinyin
zhuō

dog, canis familiaris

Pinyin
gǒu

tea

Pinyin
chá

rent, lease; rental; tax

Pinyin
zū

cup, glass

Pinyin
bēi

float, drift; tossed about

Pinyin
piào

yesterday; in former times, past

Pinyin
zuó

椅 猫

喂 苹

cat

Pinyin

māo

chair, seat

Pinyin

yǐ

artemisia; duckweed; apple

Pinyin

píng

interjection to call attention

Pinyin

wèi

Printed in Great Britain
by Amazon

13580972R00081